LAS VEGAS
THEN & NOW

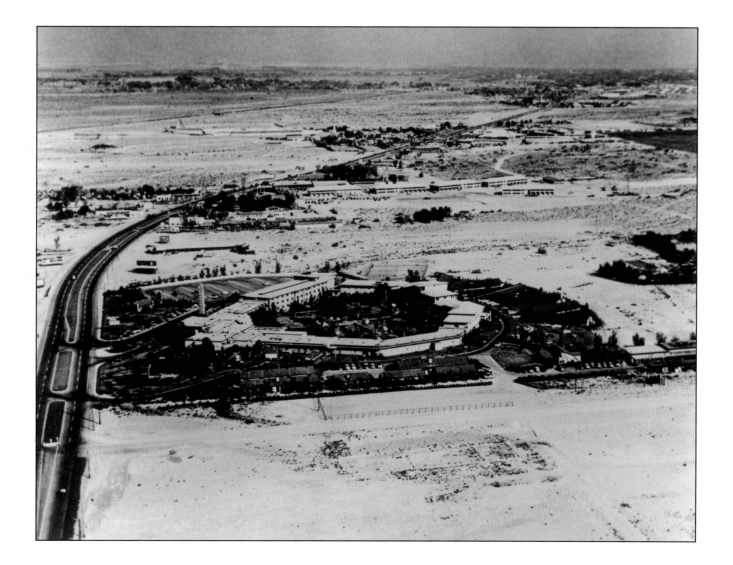

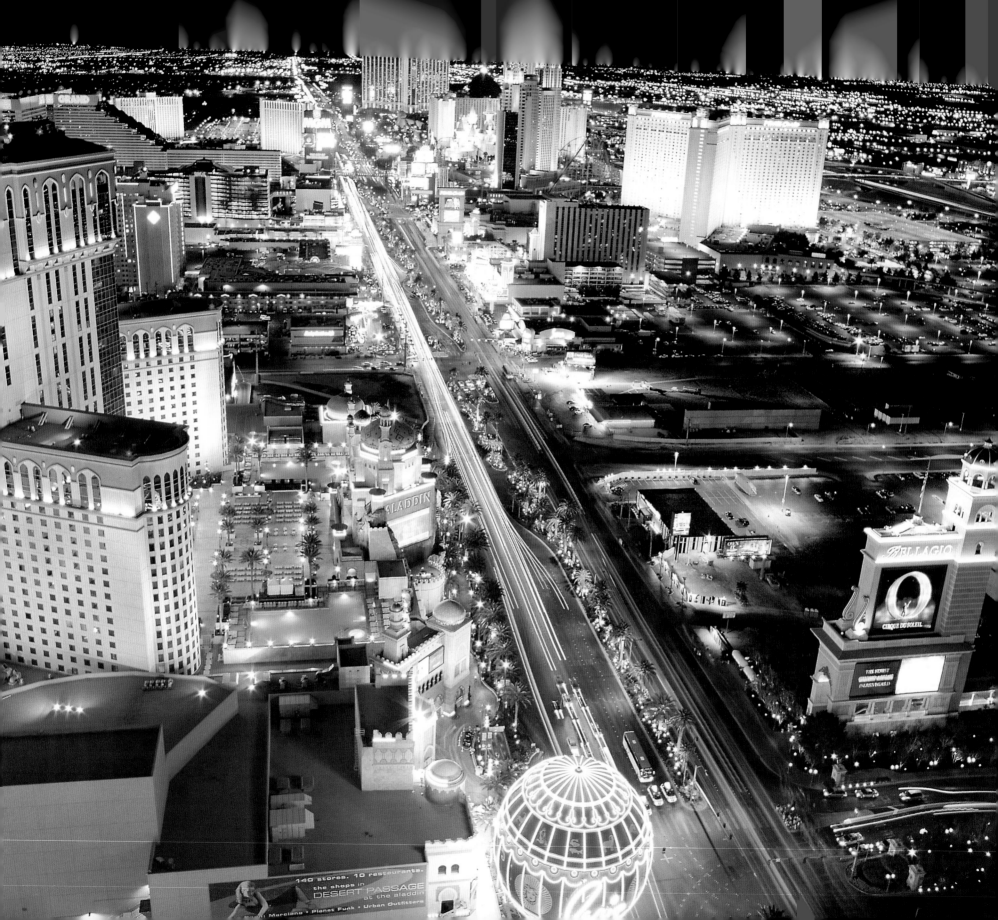

LAS VEGAS
THEN & NOW

SU KIM CHUNG

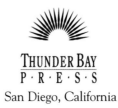

THUNDER BAY
P·R·E·S·S

San Diego, California

Thunder Bay Press
An imprint of the Baker & Taylor Publishing Group
10350 Barnes Canyon Road, San Diego, CA 92121
www.thunderbaybooks.com

Produced by Salamander Books,
an imprint of Anova Books Company Ltd.,
10 Southcombe Street, London W14 0RA, U.K.

ISBN-13: 978-1-57145-853-7
ISBN-10: 1-57145-853-0

Library of Congress Cataloging-in-Publication Data
Chung, Su Kim.
    Las Vegas then & now / Su Kim Chung.
        p. cm.
    ISBN 1-57145-853-0
    1. Las Vegas (Nev.)--Pictorial works. 2. Las Vegas (Nev.)--History--Pictorial works. I.
Title: Las Vegas then and now. II. Title.
F849.L35 C48 2002
979.3'135'00222--dc21

                                                                            2002028923

Printed in China

10 11 12 13 14 14 13 12 11 10

ACKNOWLEDGMENTS:
The author would like to thank the following people for their gracious assistance:
Kathy War, David Schwartz, Peter Michel, Frank Wright, Michael Green, Michael Gorman,
Dennis McBride, Joe Thomson, Jonnie Kennedy, Joyce Marshall, Guy Rocha, Chris Wiatrowski,
Elizabeth Warren, Chris Maciek, Greg Seymour, David Millman, Sara Jordan, Rebecca Zisch, Nanyu
Tomiyasu, Thomas Flagg, Janice Mitchell, Roger Bakke, Robert Manzanares, and Kurt Ouchida.
In addition, the publisher would like to thank Scott Tharler for his research into more recent
developments in and around Las Vegas.

INTRODUCTION

In its first hundred years, Las Vegas was transformed from a desert railroad outpost into the gambling and entertainment capital of the world. The phenomenal population growth of the past several years has added another dimension to this transformation. The ascendancy of Las Vegas as a model for the postindustrial metropolis has inspired a vigorous torrent of scholarly inquiry and social commentary from sociologists, historians, and journalists intent on uncovering the "real" Las Vegas.

The existence of Las Vegas hinges on one simple thing: water. Its harsh desert surroundings would be unlivable were it not for the natural springs that have flowed underground for centuries, creating a desert oasis in what is now the Las Vegas Valley. Unfortunately, no photographic evidence exists of what the area looked like when Spanish explorers and traders in the early nineteenth century stopped at the springs and named the site Las Vegas—"the meadows"—after the lush grass that fed on the springs. Still photographs taken at the springs in the early twentieth century provide an idea of how they may have looked when explorers such as John C. Frémont and other travelers rested there while trekking through the unforgiving Mojave Desert during the previous century.

Before long, the valley would host a more permanent settlement. In 1855, Mormon colonists from nearby Utah decided to set up a mission not far from the springs. The harsh living conditions and an unsuccessful mining venture led them to abandon the mission in 1858. Within a few years, the land they had farmed was incorporated into a ranch belonging to Octavius Decatur Gass. The property was sold to Archibald Stewart in 1882, and following Stewart's murder, his wife, Helen, successfully ran the ranch until 1902, when it was sold to the San Pedro, Los Angeles & Salt Lake Railroad. Photographs taken around this time show remnants of the original fort as it looked on the ranch property, and illustrate the starkly dramatic landscape of early Las Vegas. The driving force behind the railroad, Montana senator William Clark, carved up the property to create Clark's Las Vegas Townsite, which was auctioned off on May 15, 1905, a date that marks the birth of Las Vegas.

Contemporary photographs of the Mission-style railroad depot, ice plant, and railroad cottages illustrate how the city's existence was centered around the railroad. Other early photographs capture the frontier quality of Fremont Street, the city's main business thoroughfare, and Block 16, the city's infamous red-light district. The isolation of desert life in early Las Vegas, with its dirt streets and tumbleweeds, is also apparent in these photographs.

Images of Las Vegas in the 1920s and 1930s show a desert town that is slowly evolving into a city. The streets have been paved and are lined with graceful shade trees, and permanent public buildings such as schools and courthouses have been erected, along with luxurious private residences. The construction of Boulder Dam (later named Hoover Dam) at a site just thirty miles south of Las Vegas proved to be a significant boost to the city's economy. During the dam's construction, which spanned from 1931 to 1935, thousands of workers and their families flocked to the area, and photographs reveal how the town promoted itself as the "Gateway to Boulder Dam" to attract tourists. The legalization of gambling in 1931 would attract even more tourists, eager to fill the gambling halls and hotels that had sprung up along Fremont Street, or wanting to take advantage of Nevada's liberal marriage and divorce laws.

As the raw western gambling halls evolved into more refined casinos, neon became a popular element of signage. Photographs from the 1940s capture the most dramatic development in the history of Las Vegas—the construction of the first resort-style casino/hotels along Highway 91, the future Las Vegas Strip. Prior to 1941, this largely deserted four-mile stretch of road was home to a few small gambling clubs, but everything changed with the opening of the El Rancho Vegas that year. The combination of a casino within a luxury resort hotel was far removed from anything that existed on Fremont Street, and the El Rancho Vegas's success soon inspired others to build similar establishments along Highway 91. Although Benjamin "Bugsy" Siegel's Flamingo generally gets the most press, it was actually one of four resort hotels constructed on the Strip in the 1940s.

The 1950s saw the continued construction of Strip resorts, each one more spectacular than the last. Contemporary photographs illustrate the diverse styles of hotels such as the Desert Inn, Sahara, Sands, Riviera, and Dunes as they changed the flat desert landscape forever. The new resorts relied on entertainment even more than gambling to attract tourists in a competitive market, and the 1950s also witnessed the introduction of showgirls as featured attractions in production shows such as *Lido* and *Folies Bergere*. City officials and hotel owners were eager to market Las Vegas as a resort and convention destination in the 1950s, even promoting the atomic blasts at the nearby Nevada Test Site as a tourist attraction. The Strip's landscape changed again with the addition of Caesars Palace—a precursor of the themed megaresorts that would characterize Las Vegas hotel development in the future.

Photographs of the Strip from the mid-1970s reflect dramatic changes in the Las Vegas landscape as existing resorts replaced their bungalow-style hotels with high-rises, and the Strip's skyline slowly grew upward. Photographs of Las Vegas today reveal a downtown that is almost unrecognizable from its early days as a railroad outpost. The Strip is packed with luxury megaresorts, the result of a hotel building boom that revitalized Las Vegas in the 1990s. These photographs also capture the disappearance of public structures that have defined the city's history, and hotels that have been a reflection of its mystique and excitement. Although Las Vegas is no different from many American cities in this respect, the high-profile destruction of these structures in public implosions has given the city a reputation of having little respect for its past. Others, however, see this as just an unavoidable byproduct of a city constantly reinventing itself. Ultimately, with its glamour, its neon, its brash excess, and, yes, its tackiness, Las Vegas has captured the world's imagination. To those who are familiar with the city only through popular stereotypes, these photographs may serve as an education and a revelation. To those who live here, they may bring back nostalgia and a pride of place that Las Vegas much deserves.

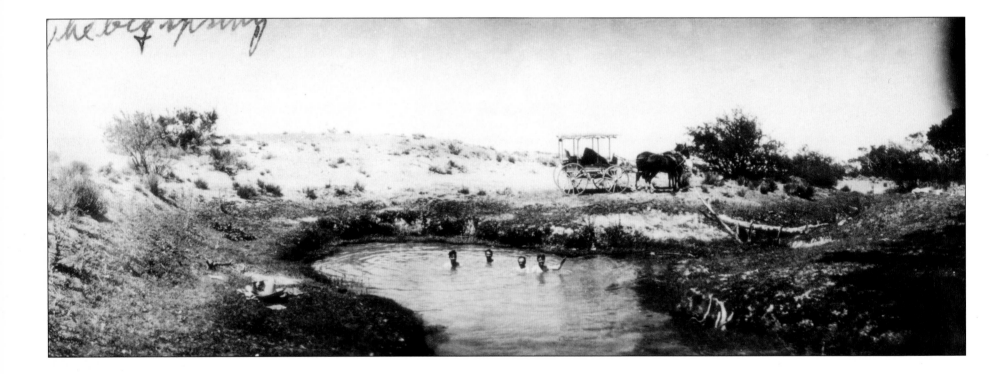

Some ten thousand years ago, underground springs erupted through the desert floor and created an oasis of lush, grassy meadows in the Las Vegas Valley. Known only to local Indian tribes for centuries, it wasn't until the 1800s that Spanish and American explorers made this natural water supply known through travel diaries and maps. The four large springs at the site fed basins such as this one, which provided a refreshing pool for visitors in the early 1900s.

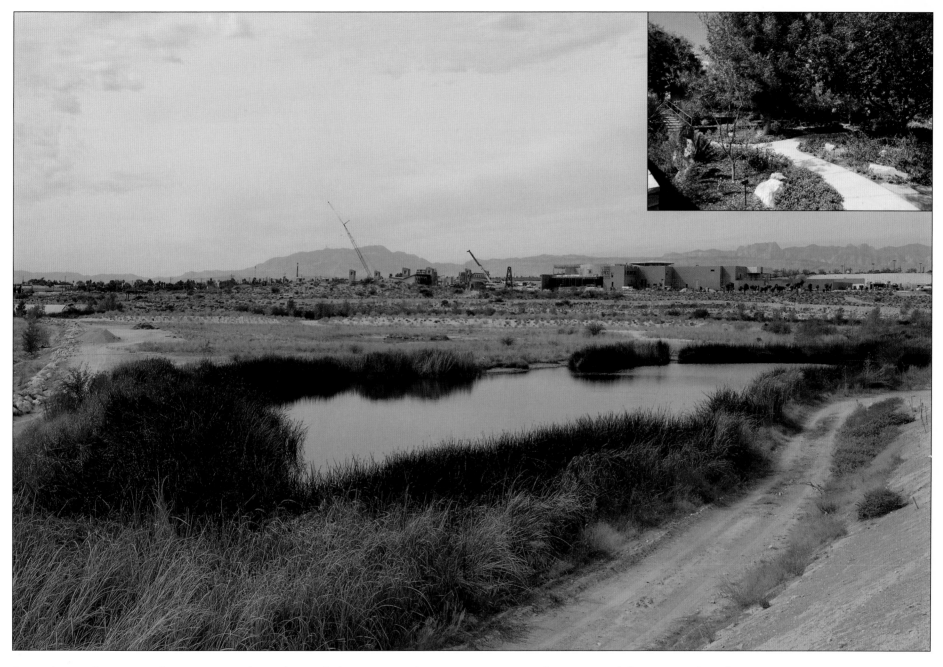

By 1950, southern Nevada's 41,000 residents demanded more ground water than nature could supply. A decade later, the population had almost tripled, worsening the problem. Despite having also tapped into nearby Lake Mead, by 1962 the Las Vegas Springs had dried up. In the 1970s, the once life-giving springs were almost paved over. But Dr. Claude Warren of the University of Nevada, Las Vegas conducted an archaeological survey that helped reroute the new expressway (I-95) around the site. In 1978,

concerned citizens and the Las Vegas Valley Water District successfully petitioned to add the springs to the National Register of Historic Places. This eventually led to the creation of the Las Vegas Springs Preserve (*inset*): a center for regional culture, wildlife, and history on the site. Composed of historical walking trails, a theater, gardens, and restored historical structures, the facility opened in June 2007.

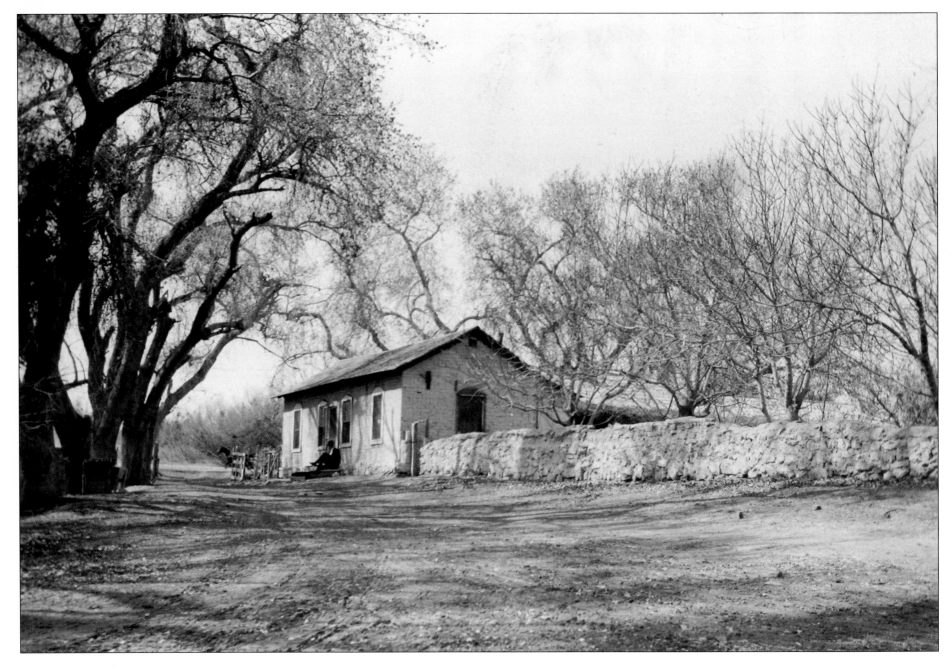

The availability of an abundant water supply in this otherwise harsh desert valley prompted Mormon missionaries from Salt Lake City to organize a Las Vegas settlement in 1855. At a site just four miles east of the Las Vegas Springs, the missionaries farmed crops and constructed an adobe fort for protection, which was later abandoned in 1858. Sections of the original fort, along with a ranch house added by later owners, are visible in this photo from the early 1900s.

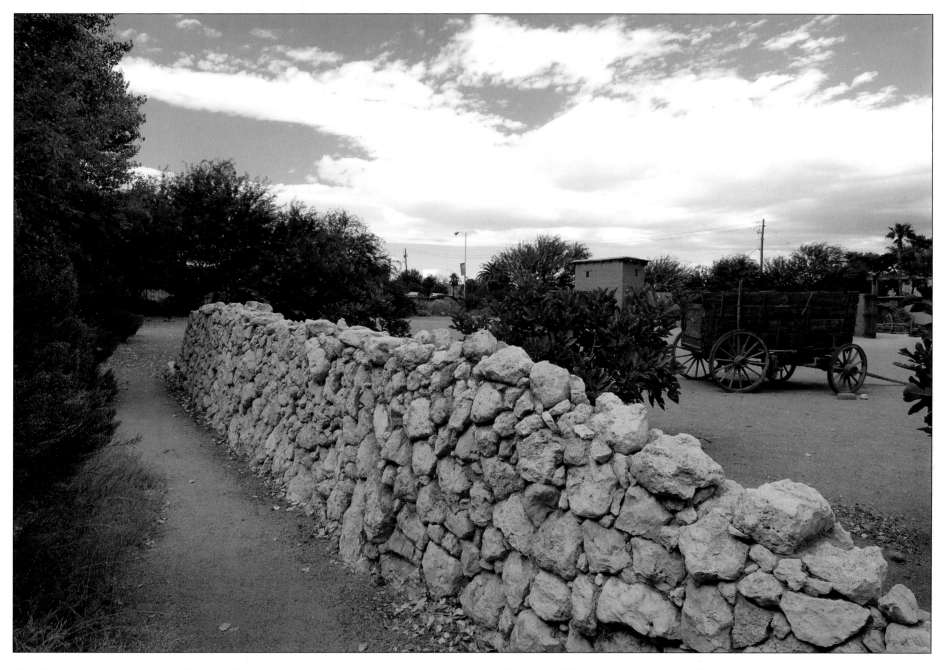

The fort later became part of the Las Vegas Rancho property that was sold to the San Pedro, Los Angeles & Salt Lake Railroad (SPLASL) in 1902. The property and the fort were then leased for various purposes over the years, until the fort's decay moved concerned citizens to have it named in the National Register of Historic Places in 1972. After a lengthy restoration, the property opened as the Old Las Vegas Mormon Fort State Historic Park in January 2000. It's the site of the oldest standing building in Nevada. The facility offers guided tours, historical reenactments, lectures, Boy Scout meetings, and archaeological activities. It's maintained by the organization Friends of the Fort, which could always use more volunteers to help preserve this important historical asset.

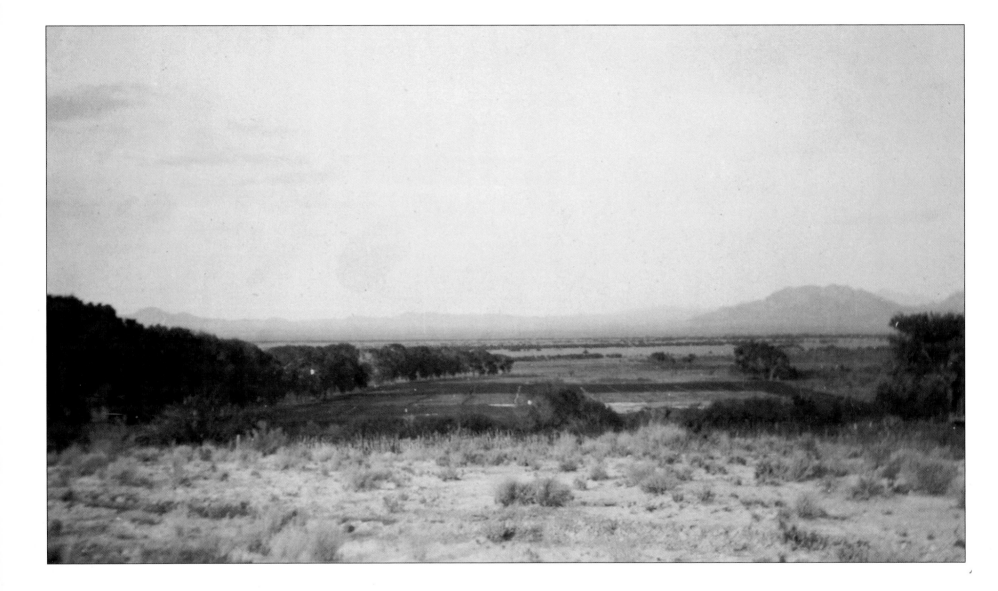

After the Mormons departed, the fort's surrounding property was farmed by O. D. Gass from 1865 to 1881. Archibald Stewart acquired the property in 1881 after Gass defaulted on a loan. After Stewart's murder in 1884, his young wife, Helen, assumed responsibility for the 1,800–2,000 acre Las Vegas Rancho. This view shows a portion of the property looking slightly northeast and to the left of Frenchmen's Mountain. The majority of this land was sold to the railroad in 1902.

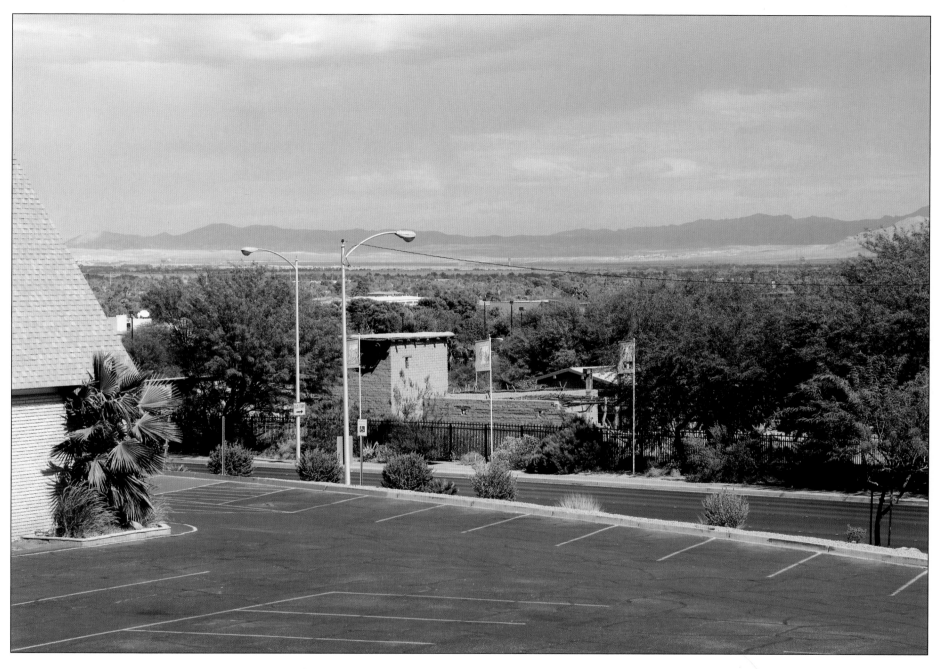

As a working ranch under Helen Stewart, the property featured cattle, fruit tree orchards, vineyards, and fields of alfalfa and grains. After it was sold to the railroad in 1902, a series of proprietors leased the land and continued to supply townsfolk with vegetables, meat, and dairy products. In the mid-1920s, some of the land on the Las Vegas Rancho was used by the United States Bureau of Reclamation for the purposes of testing cement—for use in the Hoover Dam. In 1955, the Union Pacific Railroad divided the remaining ranch property and sold it to various buyers. The Old Las Vegas Mormon Fort State Historic Park eventually became part of the Las Vegas Rancho property.

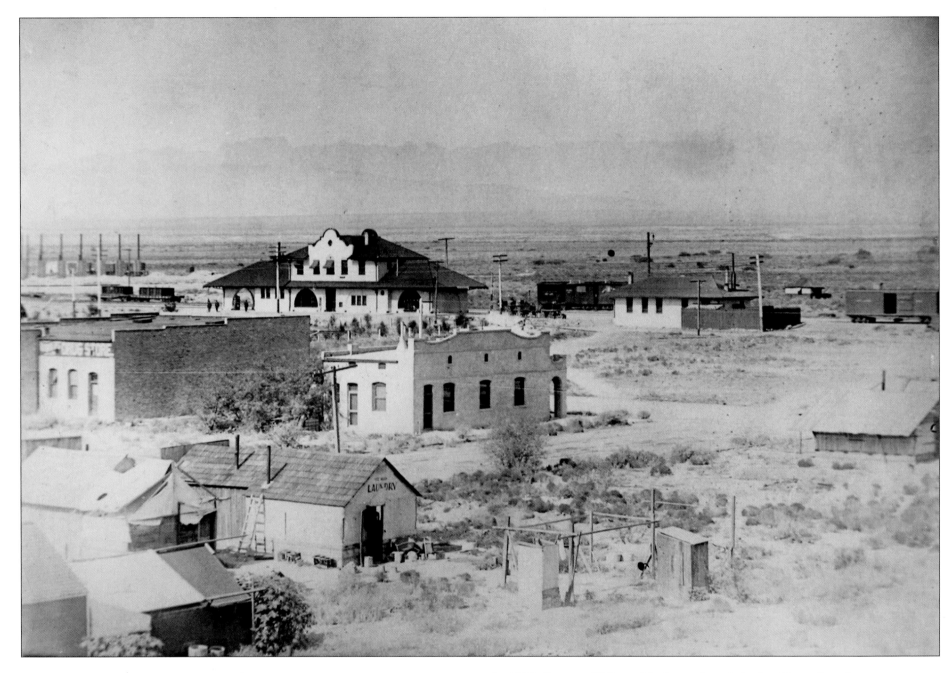

In 1902, Senator William Clark purchased the Las Vegas Rancho property on behalf of the San Pedro, Los Angeles & Salt Lake Railroad. In May 1905, the land, carved up into parcels, was auctioned off as Clark's Las Vegas Townsite. This view, looking southwest from the top of the Arizona Club in 1910, shows how quickly the town took shape. The prominent Mission-style building is the railroad depot, constructed near Fremont and Main in late 1905.

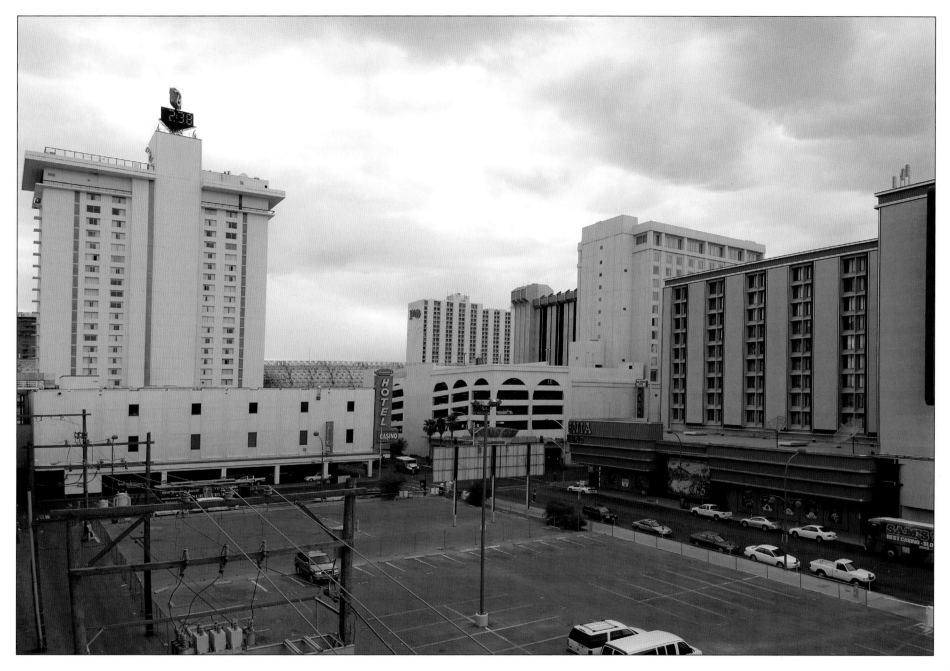

Almost a hundred years later, there are few reminders of the role the railroad played in the development of downtown Las Vegas. In the new millennium, the pronounced Plaza Hotel stands tall on the site of the original railroad depot, whose crucial historical role is all but a memory. The encroaching high-rise hotels and parking garages obscure views of the desert, once visible from all points downtown. The era of the railroad as the connector of the West ended with the rise of the motorcar and affordable air travel. But the rise of television as the connector of the nation sees no end in sight, for better or worse. In 2006, the Plaza began production of its new television program *The Hollywood Palace*.

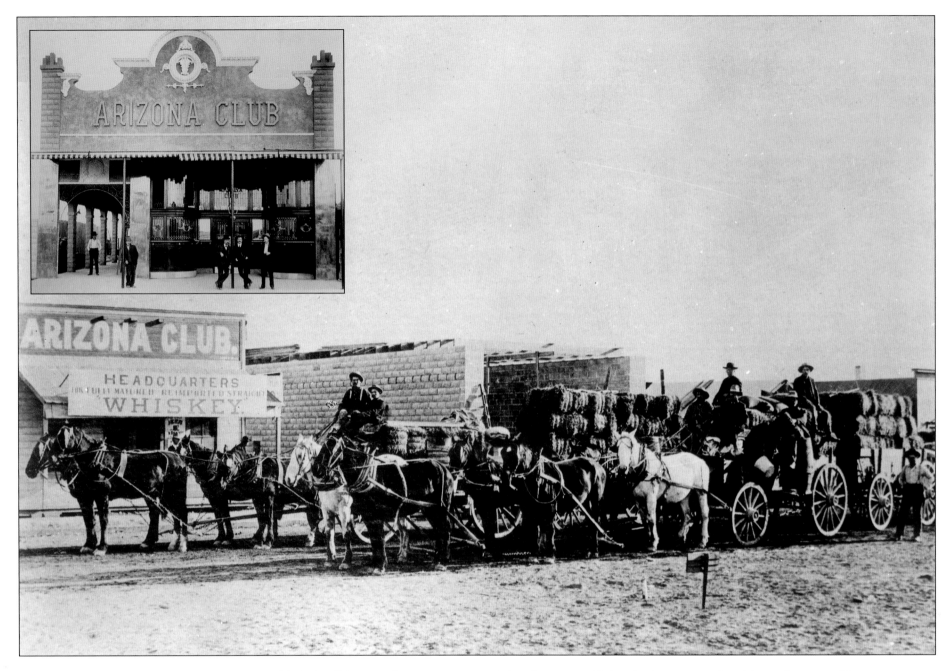

Shortly after the Las Vegas town site was established, all liquor sales were restricted to an area on First Street between Ogden and Stewart known as "Block 16." Peppered with saloons and brothels, the area soon gained an unsavory reputation as the town's red-light district. One of Block 16's most famous bars was the Arizona Club, shown here as it looked in 1905 when it was a simple wood and canvas tent with a false front. The inset shows the

updated Arizona Club, which was completed later that year. The new Arizona Club was a far cry from the crude shack it had been just months before. The club was constructed out of concrete blocks, which were considered a stylish building material at the time. In addition to its leaded glass windows, the interior featured an elegant hand-carved mahogany bar.

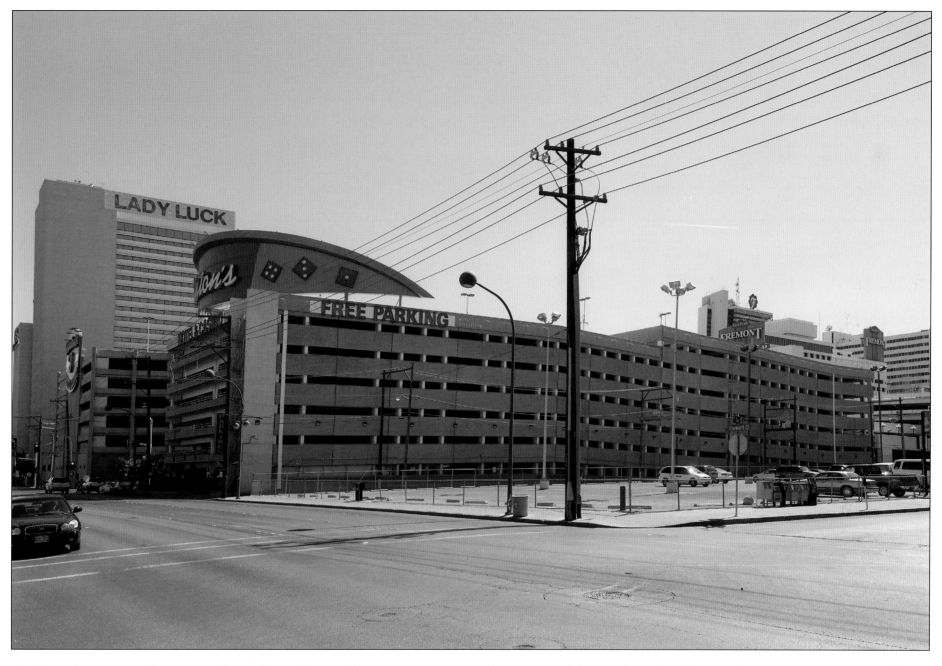

On December 1, 1941, the commanding officer of the nearby Army Air Corps Gunnery School threatened to declare Las Vegas off-limits to his men if the city didn't do something about its red-light district. The following day, local police raided the Block 16 brothels and saloons, and many, including the Arizona Club, were later shut down. Today the Binion's Horseshoe parking lot and garage rests on this infamous site. Binion's Horseshoe was the birthplace of the World Series of Poker, and some would say ground zero for the poker craze that has recently swept the United States.

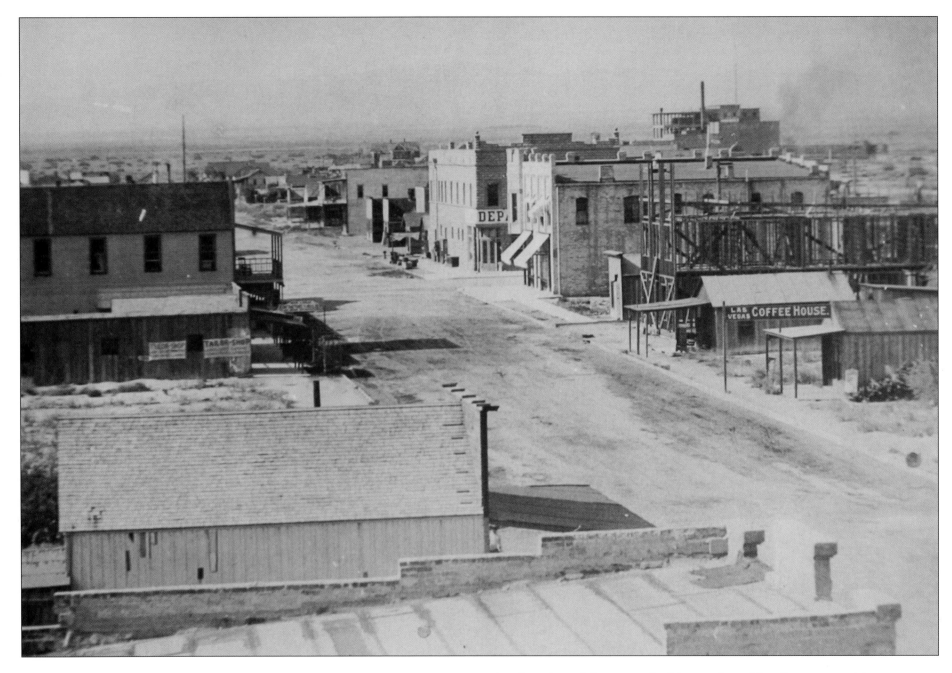

Another view of downtown looking south on First Street toward its intersection with Fremont Street in 1910 shows the pioneer character of the town. The sign marking the Thomas Department Store on the southwest corner is barely visible; it was part of the building known as the Opera House, which provided space for entertainment and meetings until it burned down in 1912.

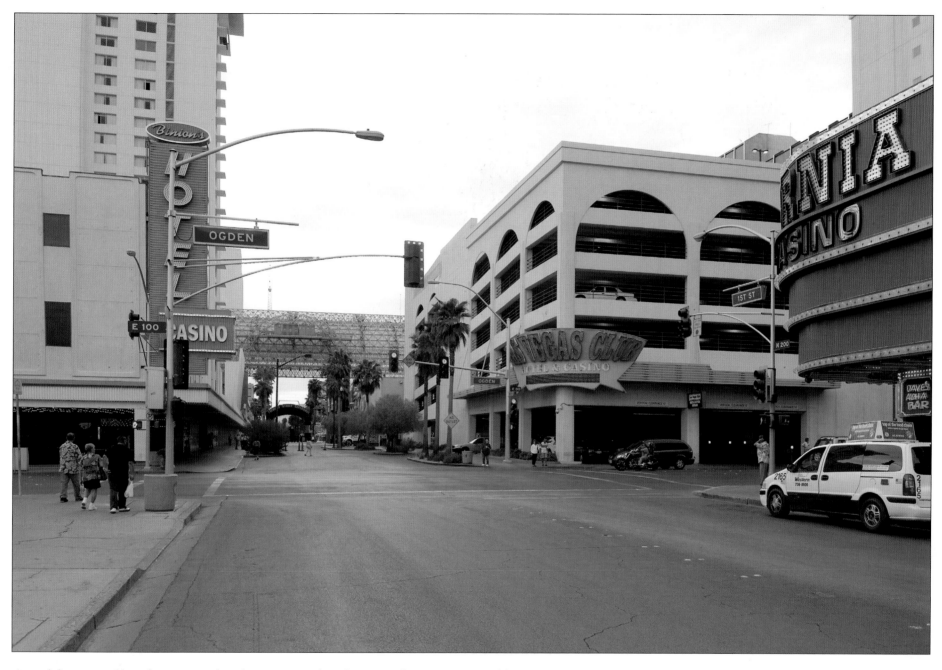

A proliferation of hotel towers and parking garages has dramatically changed the look of downtown Las Vegas, completely obscuring the view of the surrounding area. The latticed-steel "celestial vault" covering some four blocks of Fremont Street is part of the Fremont Street Experience. In addition to serving as a venue for nightly light shows, the canopy provides shade for pedestrians during the day. But more importantly, the Fremont Street Experience ensures that visitors and residents can pay homage to the part of Vegas that started it all with glitz, style, and attitude.

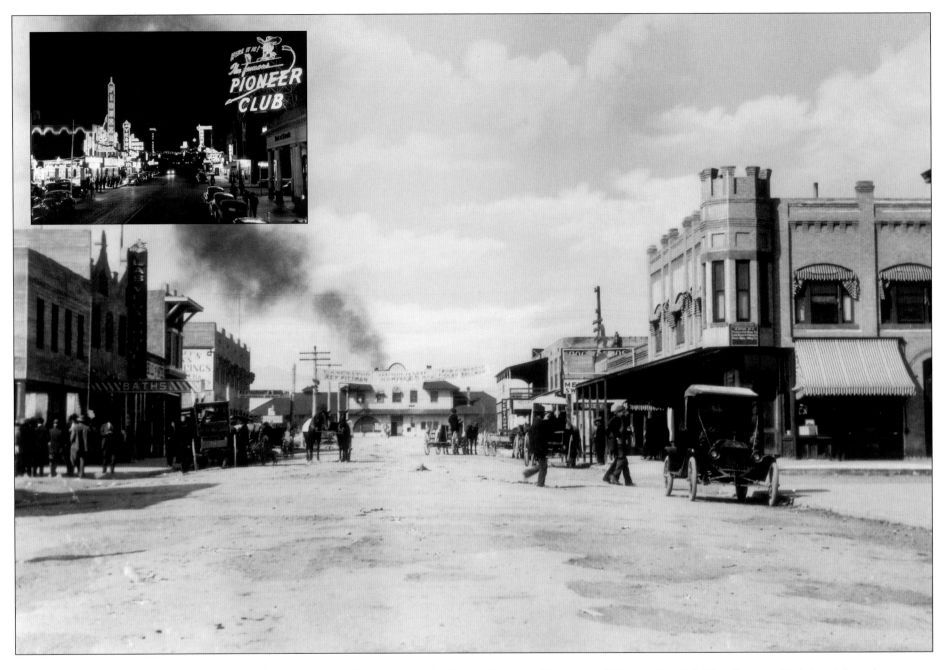

A banner proclaiming "Key Pittman for U.S. Senator" can be seen stretched across Fremont Street in this 1917 photo. Horse wagons mingle with early automobiles on unpaved streets in this view looking west from Fremont and First toward the railroad depot. The inset is a similar view, taken some thirty years later, and shows the glut of neon signs that have begun to transform Fremont Street into "Glitter Gulch." The Pioneer Club has taken the place of the Thomas Department Store at the southwest corner of First and Fremont, but its signature neon cowboy Vegas Vic would not be added to the property until 1951.

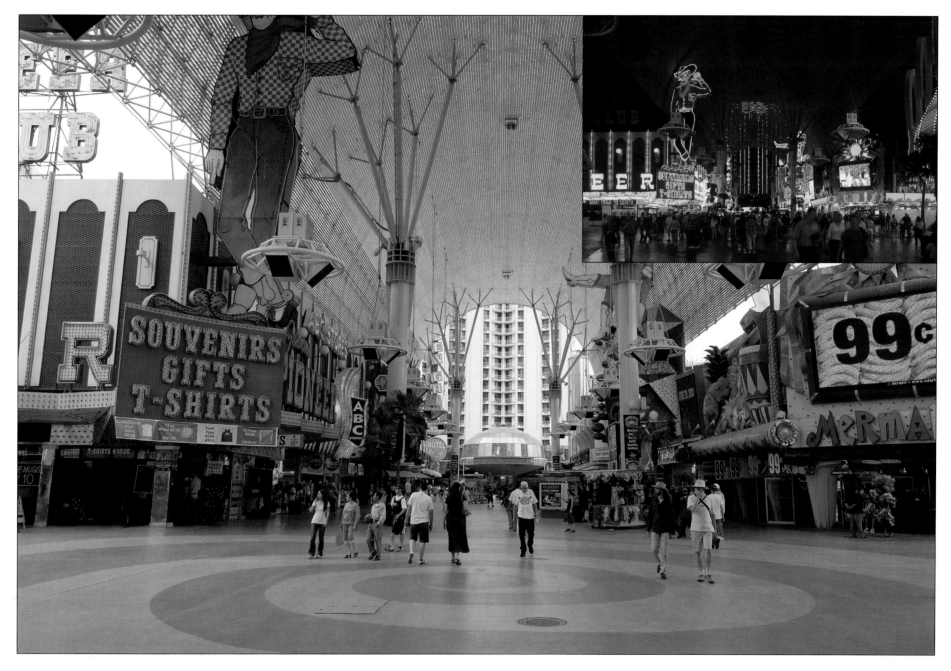

The friendly neon cowboy Vegas Vic keeps a watchful eye on the hundreds of tourists who stroll down Fremont Street on a typical day. Once bustling with traffic, it is now part of the Fremont Street Experience, a pedestrian mall that stretches from Main to Fifth Street. A collaboration between the City of Las Vegas and downtown casino owners, the project was part of a $70 million effort to revitalize downtown Las Vegas in the mid-1990s. The Experience connects businesses such as the California Hotel and Casino, Four Queens, Golden Nugget, Golden Gate, Fitzgerald's, Fremont, Las Vegas Club, Main Street Station, and Binion's Gambling Hall and Hotel. The Pioneer Club today deals kitsch rather than cards as one of the most popular souvenir shops in Vegas.

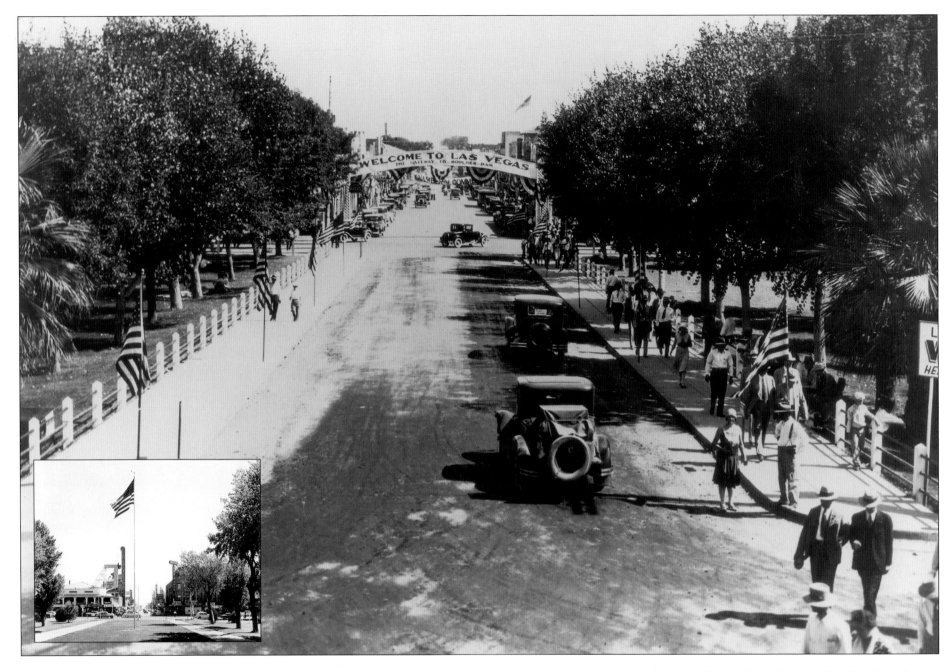

In this view looking east on Fremont Street from the tree-lined park in front of the railroad depot around 1930, the banner welcoming new arrivals to Las Vegas proudly declares the city as "The Gateway to Boulder Dam." Twenty years later (*see inset*), the park is still there, minus a few trees, but the banner is gone and the skyline over Fremont Street is crammed with distinctive neon signs.

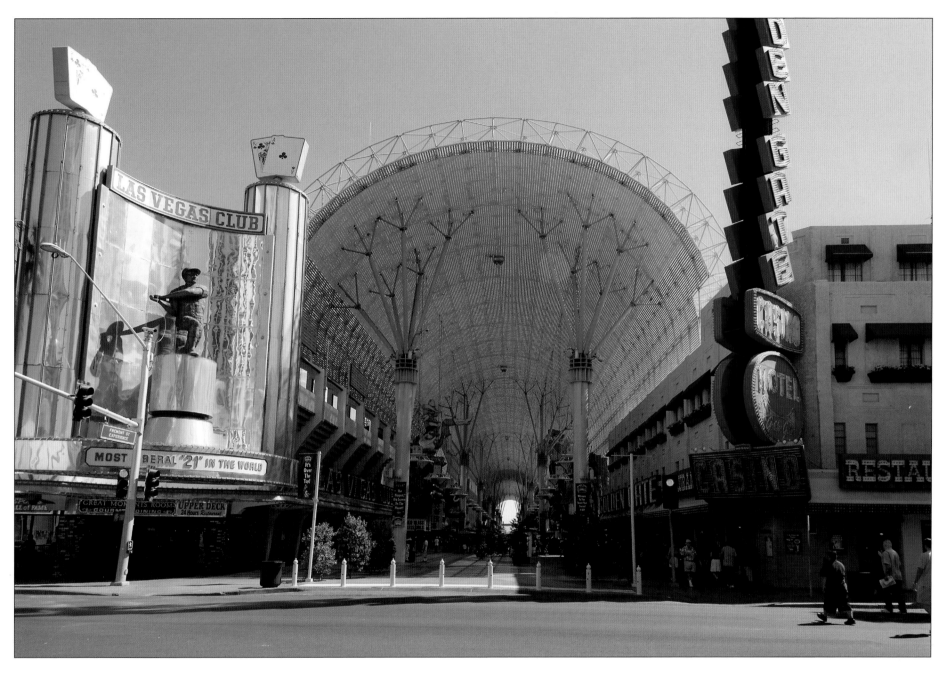

In this contemporary view looking east on Fremont Street from the Plaza Hotel, the railroad station and its tranquil park are long gone and the ninety-foot-high Fremont Street canopy is a prominent sight. Hovering over four blocks and ten casino-hotels, the latticed-steel canopy serves as both daytime shelter and nighttime display. When the desert sun goes down, a spectacular computer-generated light show sweeps across the concave underbelly of the 1,400-foot-long structure. During each six-minute show, a state-of-the-art, 540,000-watt, concert-quality sound system pumps through more than 200 speakers. In June 2004, a $17 million upgrade by LG Electronics helped boost the attraction's visual technological capabilities to include over 12.5 million synchronized LED modules. Countless movies have been shot at the Experience, as well as episodes of *CSI: Crime Scene Investigation*, the Travel Channel, and National Geographic.

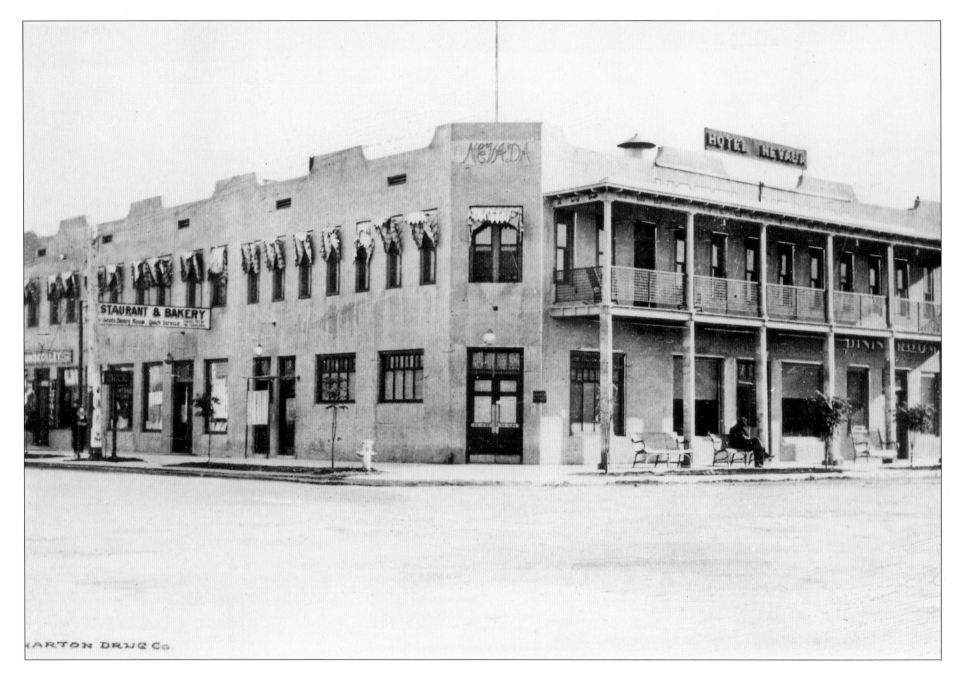

The Hotel Nevada was built in January 1906, and a year later the first telephone in Las Vegas was installed at the hotel in the office of Charles "Pop" Squires. Squires, a true Las Vegas pioneer who arrived in 1905, played many important roles in early Las Vegas, but was probably best remembered as editor of the *Las Vegas Age* newspaper. The hotel was later enlarged and renamed the Sal Sagev ("Las" and "Vegas" spelled backward) in 1931.

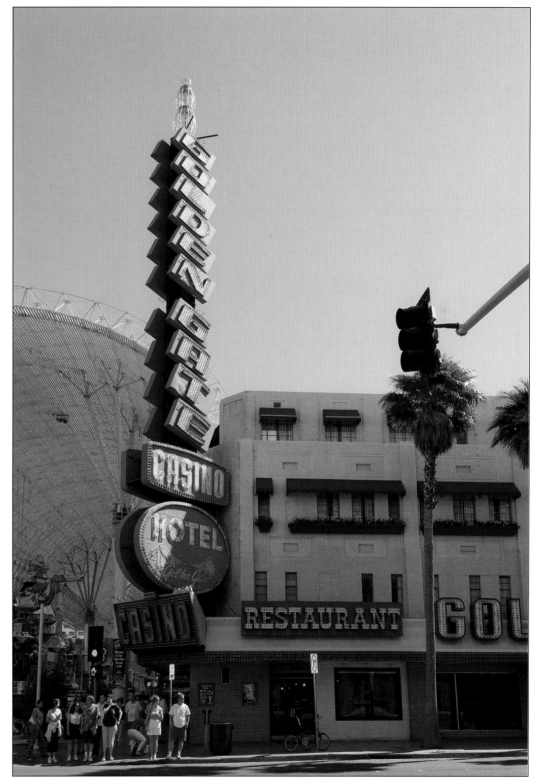

In 1955, the Golden Gate began operating as a casino underneath the Sal Sagev Hotel. By 1974, it had become successful enough to assume the entire operation and the property was renamed the Golden Gate Hotel. Today, this historic property still features many original wood fixtures from its earlier incarnations and, with only 106 rooms, it is the smallest hotel on Fremont Street. The building underwent a major restoration in 1990, bringing back some of the building's original historical luster. In 1991, the Golden Gate served its 25 millionth shrimp cocktail at an elaborate celebration that included the four mayors whose terms spanned the hotel's years of shrimp-cocktail service. Over 2.1 million lights give today's Golden Gate its glow.

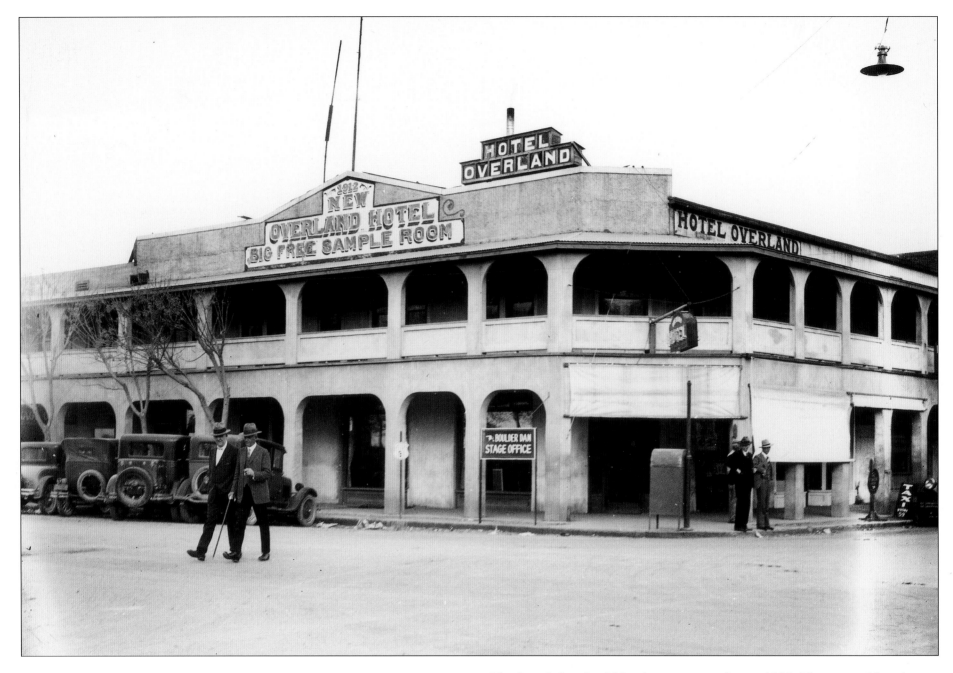

The "new" Overland Hotel as it appeared circa 1930. The original hotel, built in 1906, burned down in 1911. The curious sign proclaiming "Big Free Sample Room" referred to a room where salesmen could display their wares (not a free hotel room), and was a precursor to those provided to modern convention vendors.

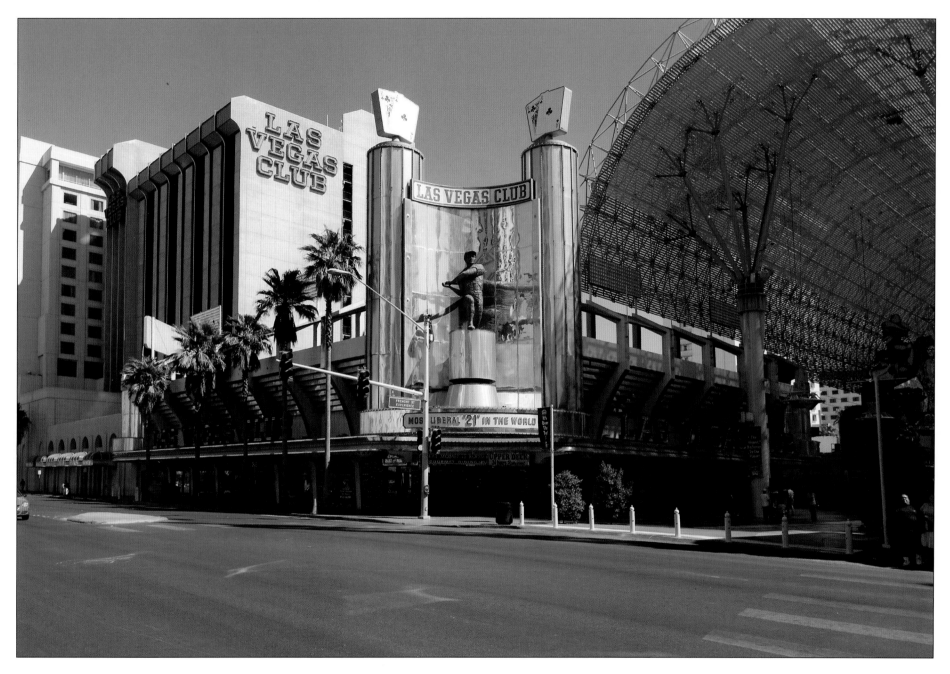

The Overland Hotel became the Las Vegas Club in 1931 when legalized gambling returned to Nevada. For many years it featured the tallest neon sign (120 feet) on Fremont Street. Its current facade reflects the hotel's sports-themed casino design. The Las Vegas Club's Sports Hall of Fame reportedly features the most complete collection of baseball memorabilia outside of Cooperstown, New York. In addition to all the sports mementos, the casino is known for dealing "the most liberal 21 in the world," based on its lenient player-oriented blackjack rules on splitting, doubling down, and winning on any six-card total under 21.

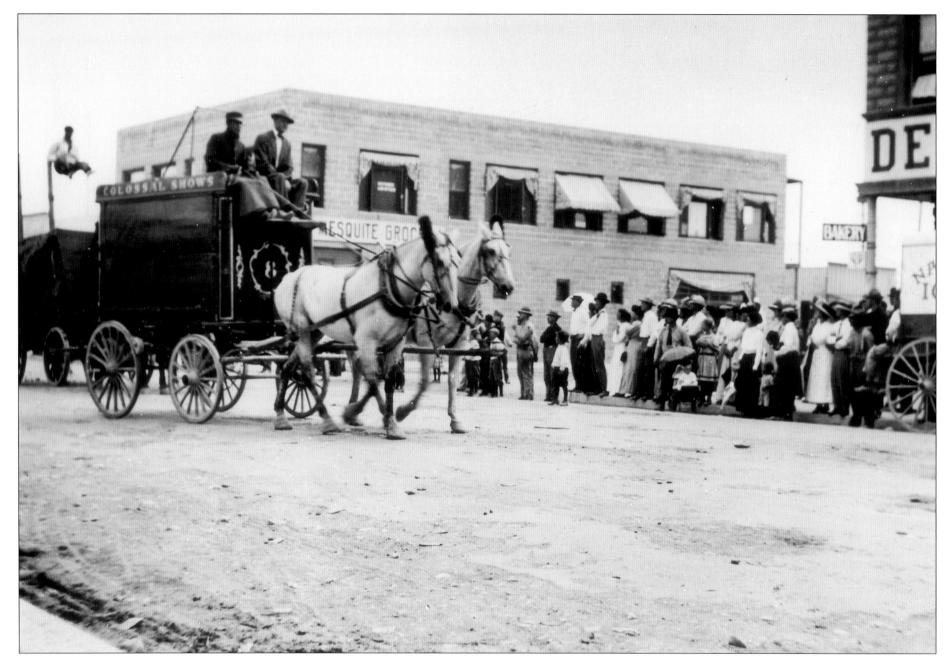

In September 1911, the Colossal Circus came to town and paraded up Fremont Street. With crowds of bystanders watching from the sidewalk next to Thomas Department Store, acrobats performed while on a moving wagon. Located across the street on the southeast corner of Fremont and First is the Mesquite Grocery Store.

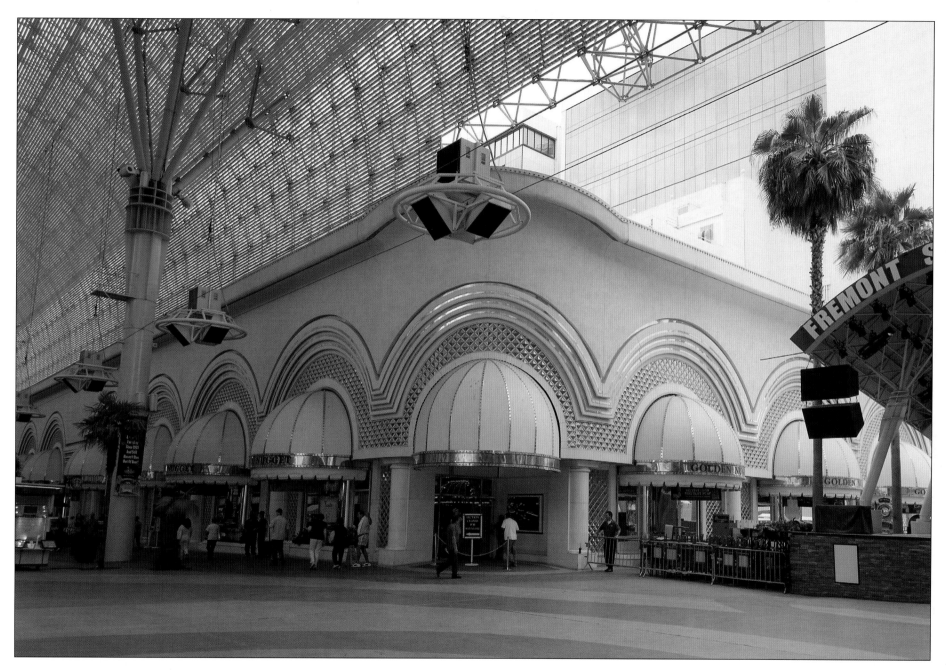

The modest concrete buildings have disappeared and the dirt streets were paved in 1925. Twenty-one years later, the Golden Nugget first appeared on the southeast corner of First and Fremont, with a Barbary Coast–style interior that made it downtown's most stylish gambling hall. The world's largest known gold nugget—the eighteen-inch, sixty-pound "Hand of Faith"—was discovered in Australia in 1981 and put on display near the grand entrance of the Golden Nugget. Decades later in January 2004, during a two-year, $30 million renovation, Travelscape.com founders Tim Poster and Tom Breitling acquired the Golden Nugget properties in both Las Vegas and Laughlin from MGM Mirage, Inc. Hoping to capitalize on the poker craze, the Golden Nugget hit the small screen in May 2005 with the National Heads-Up Poker Championship, which aired on NBC. In October of 2006 its *Cover Girls* variety show from London made headlines with its blend of dancing, singing, comedy, and three-dimensional imagery.

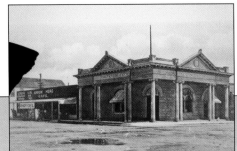

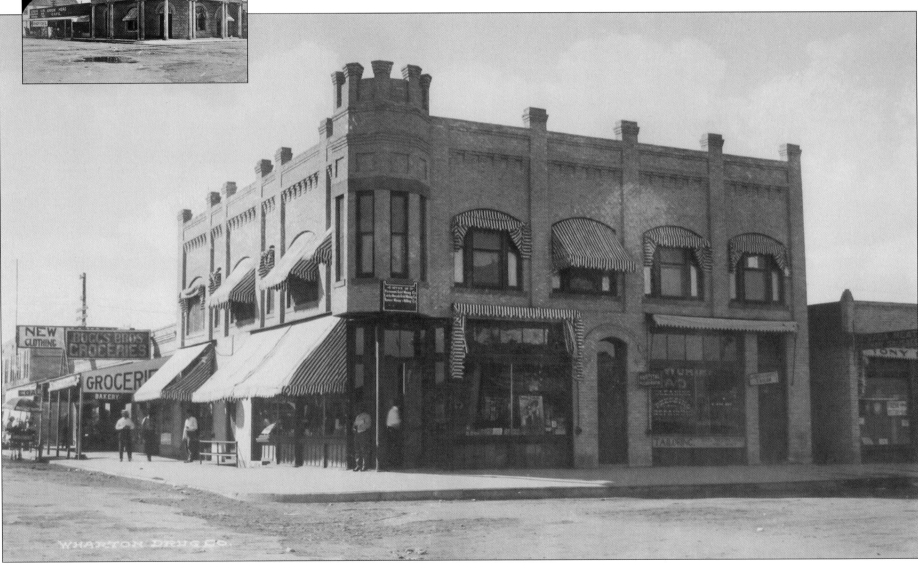

The Las Vegas Pharmacy, shown here around 1917, occupied the first floor of this castlelike structure on the northwest corner of First and Fremont. From about 1906 to 1920, the upper story served as a twelve-bed hospital and was run by Dr. Roy Martin. Just opposite the Las Vegas Pharmacy, on the northeast corner, was the First State Bank (*see inset*), the second bank to open in Las Vegas, which is shown here as it looked shortly after its completion in January 1906. Solidly constructed out of concrete blocks, the building featured a classical facade and an interior that included marble floors and mahogany wood fixtures.

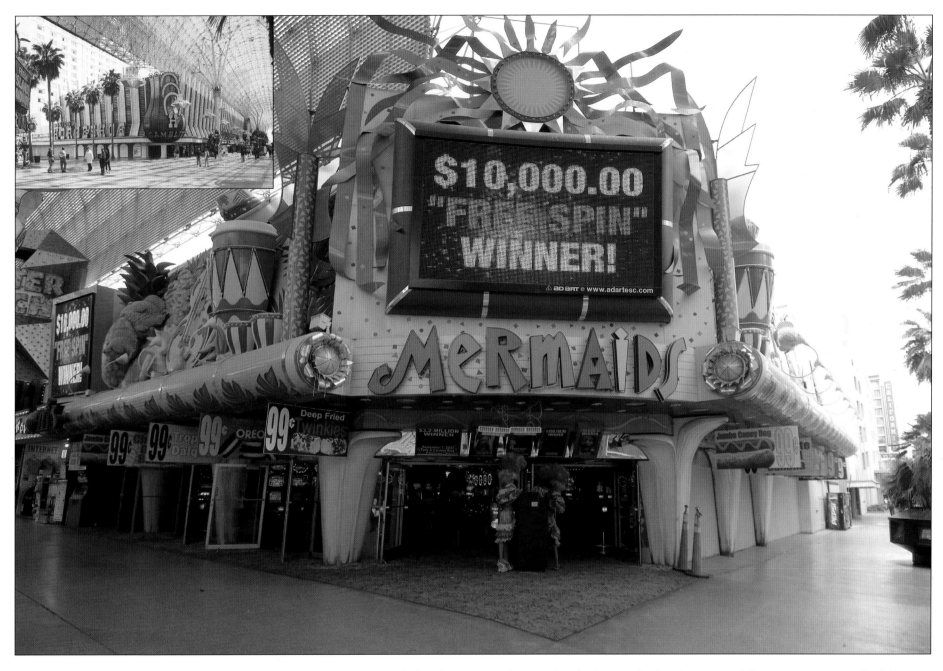

The Las Vegas Pharmacy closed around 1955 and was then remodeled and replaced by a succession of small casinos. It operated as Sassy Sally's for many years until the late 1990s, when it was replaced by the Jules Verne–themed Mermaids Casino. The historic First State Bank was demolished in 1958 to make way for the Bird Cage Club, which was later absorbed by the Mint Casino. A 1965 expansion added the twenty-six-story tower and spectacular pink neon facade that made the Mint one of downtown's most colorful casinos. In 1988, the Mint was purchased by and absorbed into its next-door neighbor Binion's Horseshoe (*see inset*). In 2004, Binion's and its popular poker brand were bought by Harrah's but retained the Horseshoe identity; today it is owned by MTR.

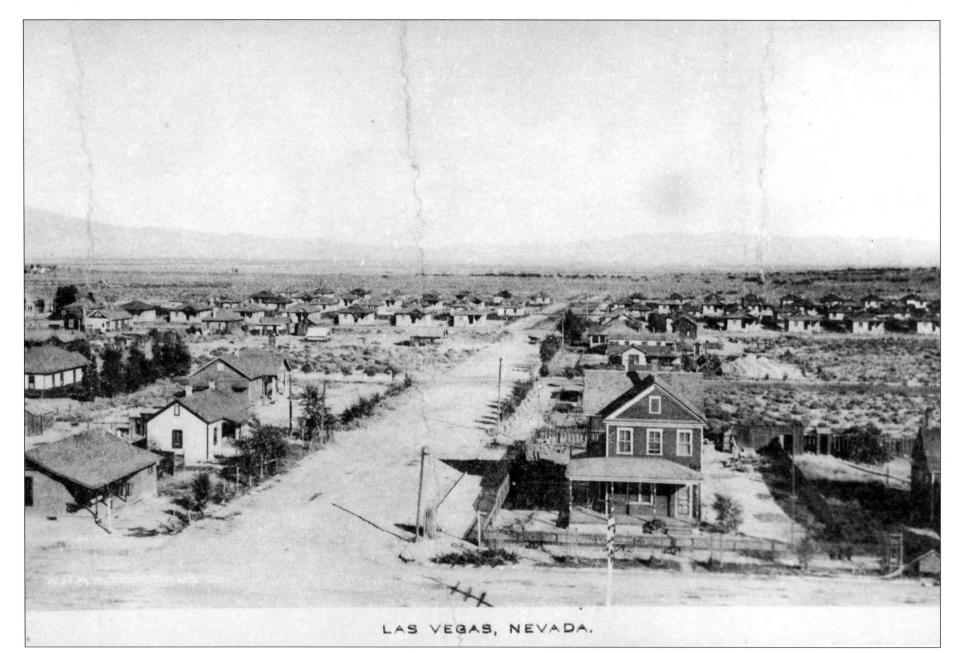

LAS VEGAS, NEVADA.

This is the view looking east from Main and Bonneville around 1910. Tidy rows of railroad cottages are clustered on either side of Bonneville from Second Street to Fourth Street. The town ends at Fifth Street, surrounded only by desert and mountains, and the isolation of living in early Las Vegas is dramatically apparent.

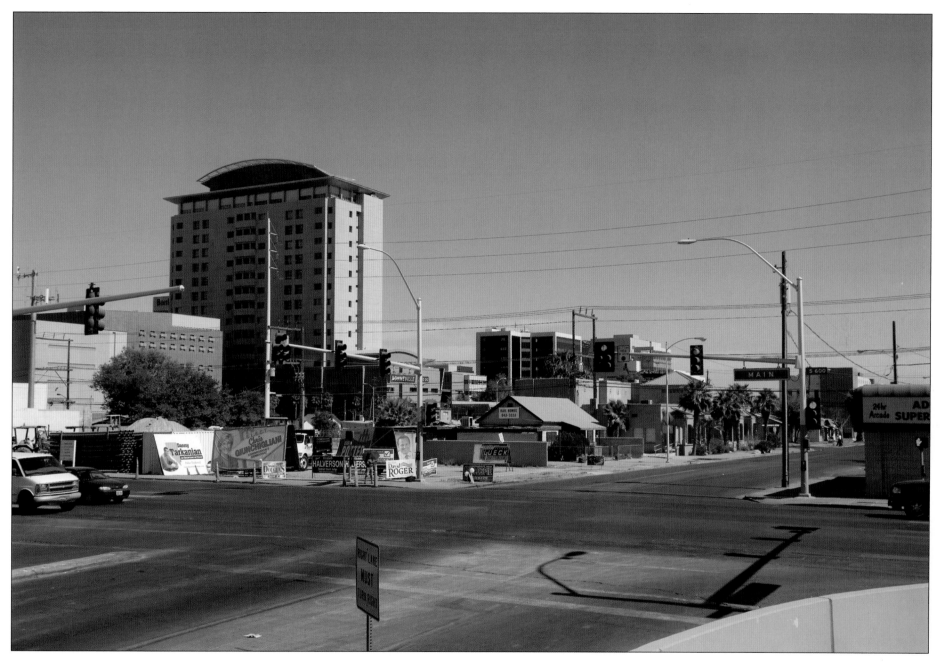

Time and progress have erased the frontier character of the town and most of the railroad cottages are long gone. The desert landscape that once surrounded the tiny town has been pushed back by development on all sides, and is no longer visible. Prominent in the background is the eight-story Lloyd D. George U.S. Courthouse, dedicated on November 1, 2000.

That isolated feeling is also a thing of a past, and the town itself has enough people to make one forget its inherent desert landscape. Vegas stretches far beyond Fifth Street (Las Vegas Boulevard), encompassing twenty-five square miles and growing every year, with a current population of around 65,000—more than 20 percent of Nevada's total population.

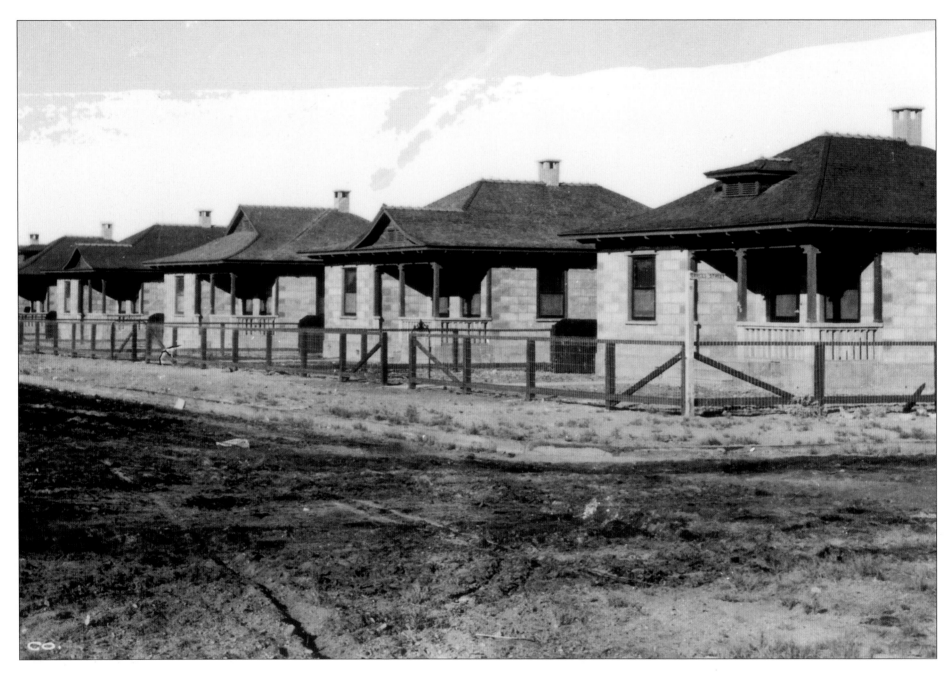

From 1909 to 1911, the SPLASL Railroad constructed numerous railroad cottages to house railroad workers and their families. The cottages, such as those shown here at the corner of Third and Garces, were constructed in the bungalow style out of concrete blocks and wood frames. Each employee cottage cost approximately $1,700 to build, and the railroad charged families rent of $20 a month for a four-bedroom house.

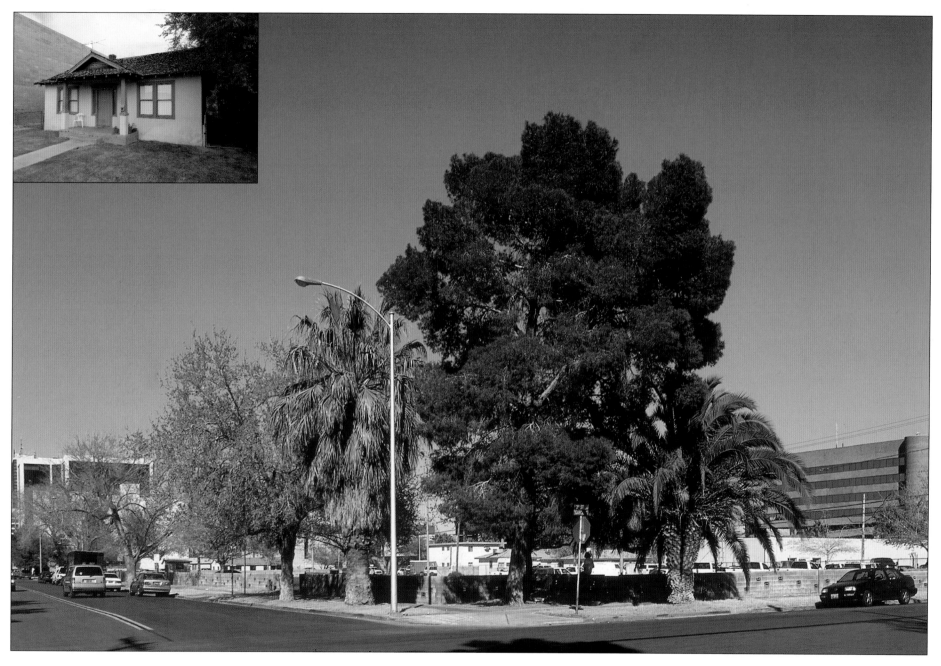

The railroad cottages at Third and Garces are long gone and, of the sixty-four original cottages built between 1909 and 1911, only a dozen remain (*inset*). Most are located near a stretch of Casino Center Boulevard (formerly Second Street), and it is likely that seven of these may soon be razed to make way for commercial development. In April 2002, the Preserve Nevada organization added the historic Railroad Cottage District to its list of "Ten Most Endangered Sites." There's nothing left of SPLASL on the spot today, nor in many other places either. In 1916, it changed its name to the Los Angeles & Salt Lake and eventually became just another asset gobbled up by the largest railroad in America, the Union Pacific. Today UP has enough track miles to circle the moon approximately five times.

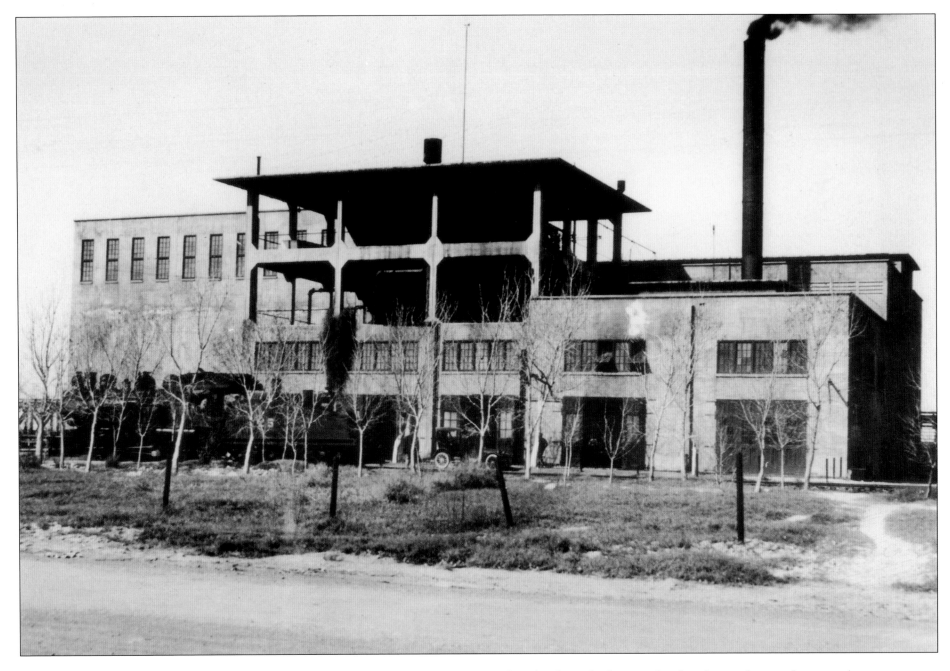

Before the days of refrigerated railroad cars, the ice plant was the most important building in Las Vegas, as it enabled produce to be shipped across the desert without fear of spoilage. The original plant had burned down in 1907, leaving the town without this precious commodity until the new plant, shown here, was completed in April 1908. Constructed out of reinforced concrete, it was the only icing station between San Bernardino, California, and Salt Lake City, Utah.

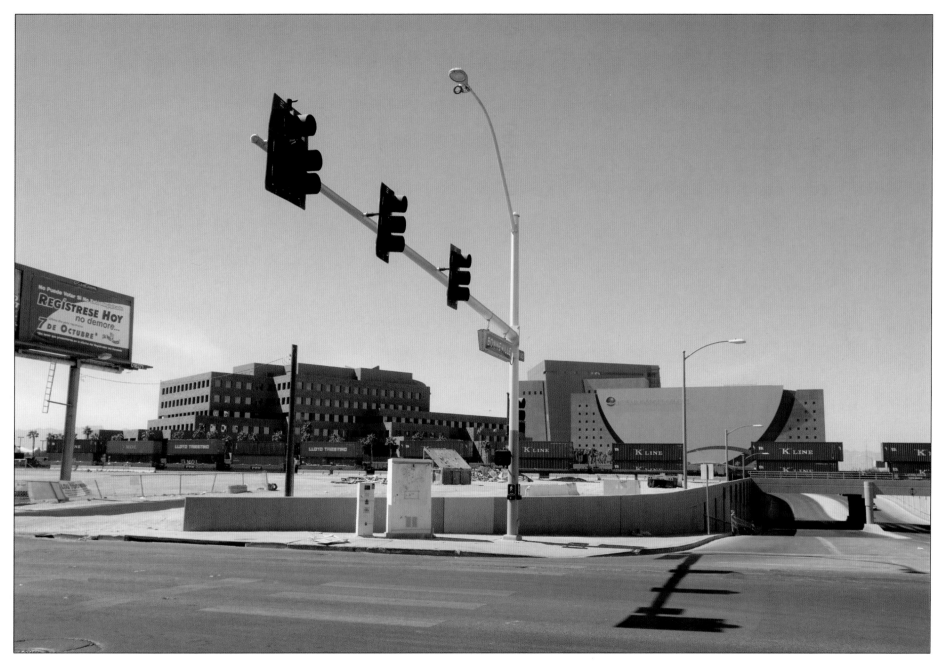

After its role in supplying ice for railroad cars ended, the ice plant continued to produce ice on a commercial basis for casinos, restaurants, and grocery stores for many years. By 1983, the building was vacant, and despite diligent efforts by local preservationists, it was declared unsafe and demolished in May 1988. The approximate site of the icehouse now features the popular Ice House

Lounge. This $5 million Art Deco structure is where the beautiful people go to see and be seen among the thumping music, modern decor, plasma televisions, and solid-ice bar tops. The inside of the Ice House Lounge showcases historical Las Vegas photography, including the old original ice plant.

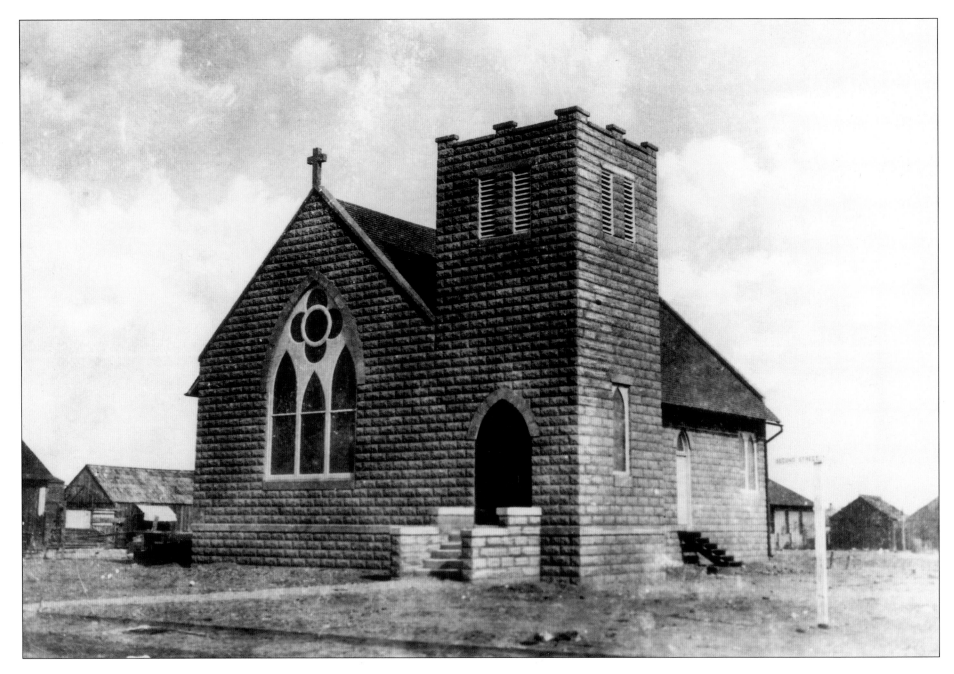

The charming Christ Church Episcopal on the northeast corner of Second and Carson is shown here shortly after its completion in 1908. Founding members included Las Vegas pioneers Delphine "Mom" and Charles "Pop" Squires, who were present at the laying of the cornerstone. Other early Las Vegas churches included the First Methodist at Third and Bridger and the St. Joan of Arc Catholic Church, which were founded in 1905 and 1910, respectively.

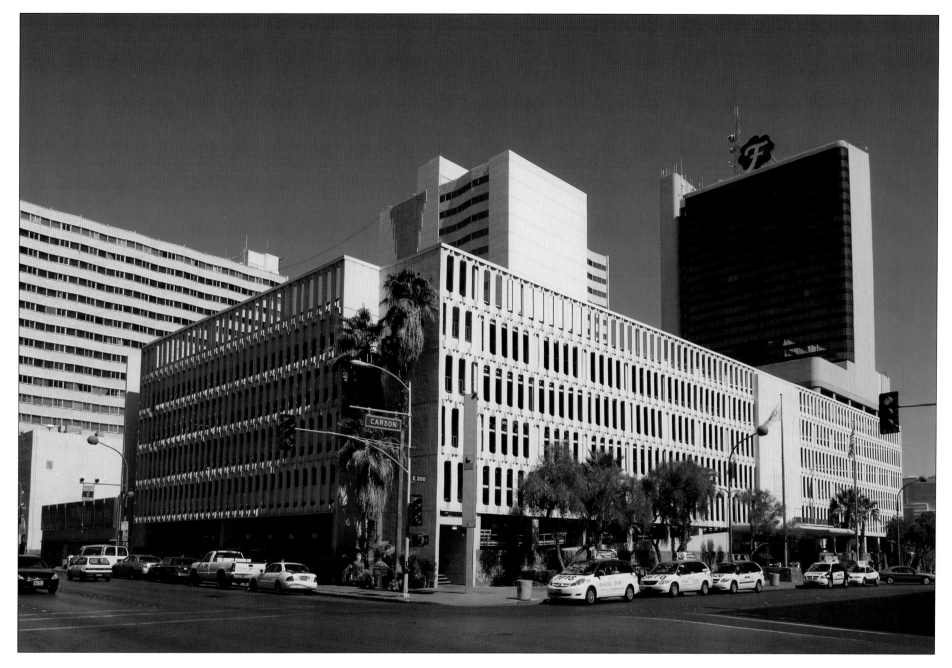

By 1953, Christ Church officials realized that they had outgrown their downtown location. A generous property gift enabled them to construct a new church at its current location on Maryland Parkway and St. Louis, and the sale of the downtown property provided funds to purchase additional property for adequate parking at the new location. The original building was destroyed soon afterward. Today, the site houses a municipal parking garage that's just a stone's throw away from the Fremont Street Experience and the Four Queens Hotel and Casino. You don't hear much preaching at the Four Queens, but you can always get a service—the hotel has eight restaurants, including a cigar lounge, pizza joint, and the romantic Hugo's Cellar.

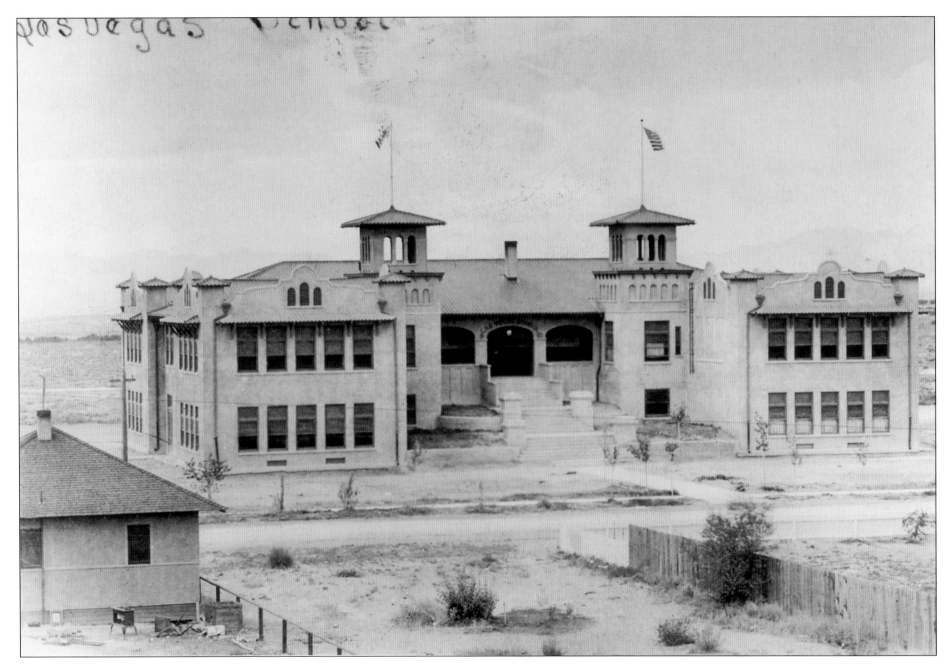

This two-story building housed the Las Vegas Grammar School and Clark County High School, which opened at Fourth and Bridger in October 1911. The Mission-style building featured a heating plant and electric fan ventilation, and was a vast improvement over the three-room wooden schoolhouse on Second and Lewis that had burned down in December 1910. The high school was moved to a building at Fourth and Clark in December 1917.

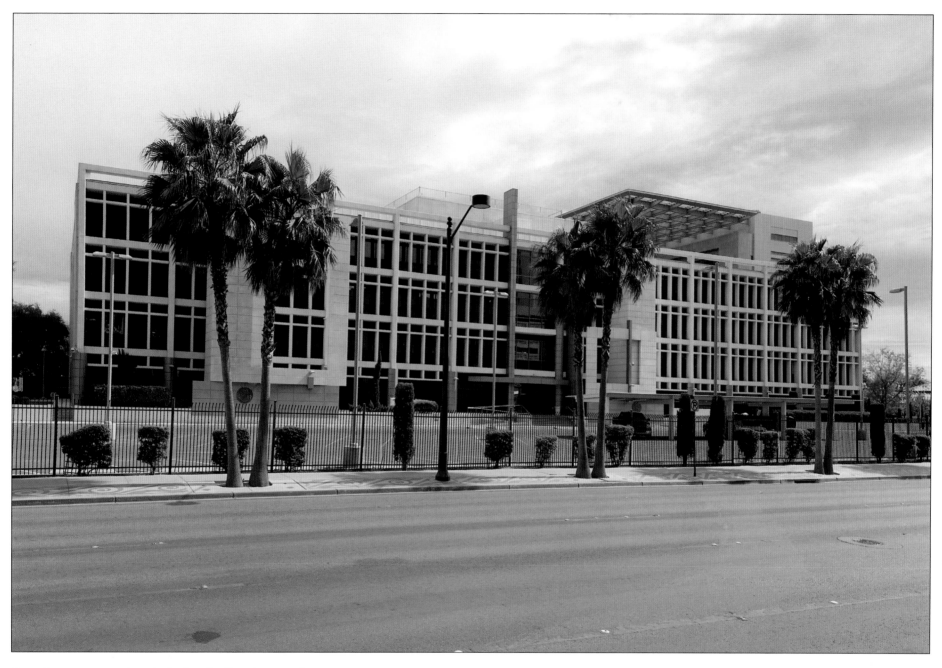

By 1921, overcrowding led school officials to authorize construction on two additional buildings near the Las Vegas Grammar School. The following year, a kindergarten building and a manual arts building were constructed on the Fourth and Bridger site. In 1964, the three buildings were sold to the U.S. government and demolished to make way for the present Foley Federal Building on Las Vegas Boulevard (formerly Fifth Street). The architect of this deal was Reed Whipple, a Mormon who cleared up the red tape that once prohibited the land from service for any purpose other than educational. While no longer a school, it's still a place of learning and expression. The building has hosted nuclear protests, bankruptcy trials, and civil-rights lawsuits.

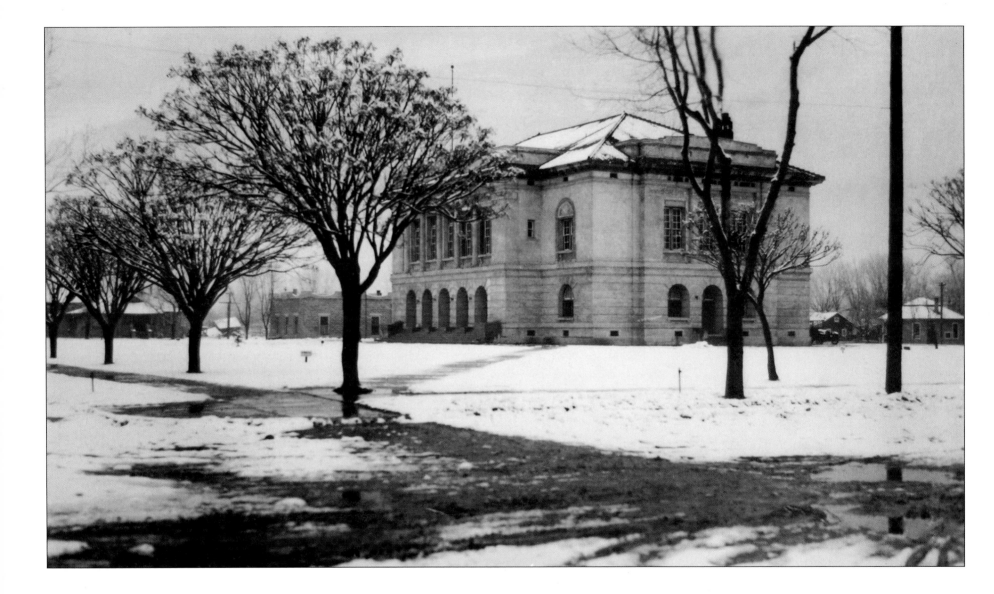

Dedicated in December 1914, the Clark County Courthouse was the work of prominent Nevada architect Frederick J. DeLongchamps. The building was designed in a Spanish Colonial Revival style and situated in the center of the courthouse square near the southeast corner of Second and Carson. The tree-shaded lawn surrounding the courthouse is slightly obscured here due to a rare Las Vegas snowstorm in the 1940s.

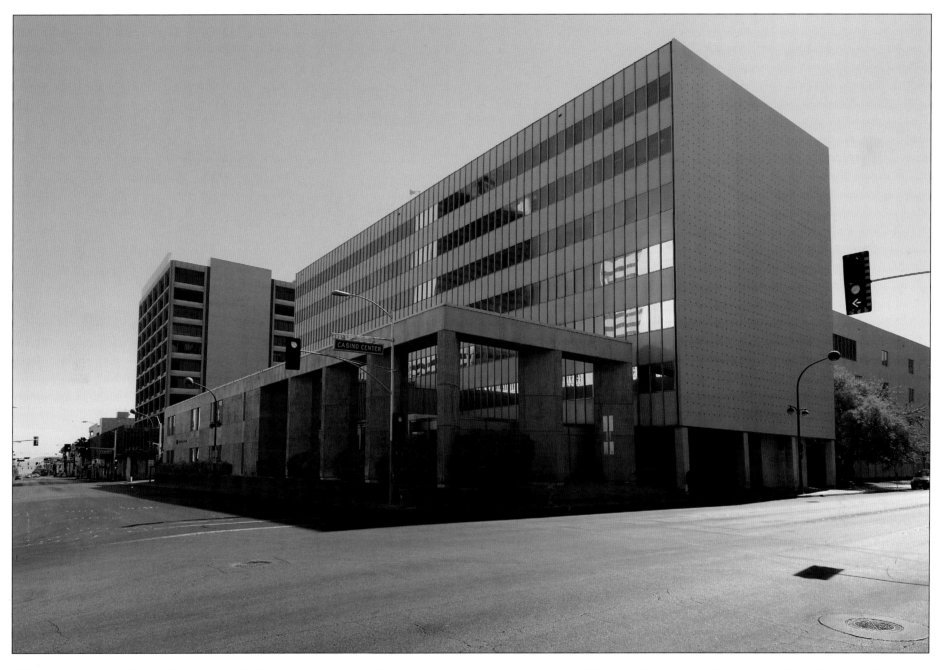

Glass, concrete, and steel characterize the International style of the current Clark County Courthouse, designed by local architects Walter Zick and Harris Sharp in 1958. Although the original DeLongchamps structure stood next to it briefly, it was demolished soon afterward. In the 1980s, Clark County officials remodeled Zick and Sharp's original design with a two-story concrete addition and colonnade done in the Brutalist style. Today, the courthouse stands as the steward of a worldwide phenomenon: the Las Vegas wedding. Each year, over 130,000 couples hold a Vegas wedding, making it the wedding capital of the world. On holidays, the Clark County Courthouse is open twenty-four hours a day to handle the capacity.

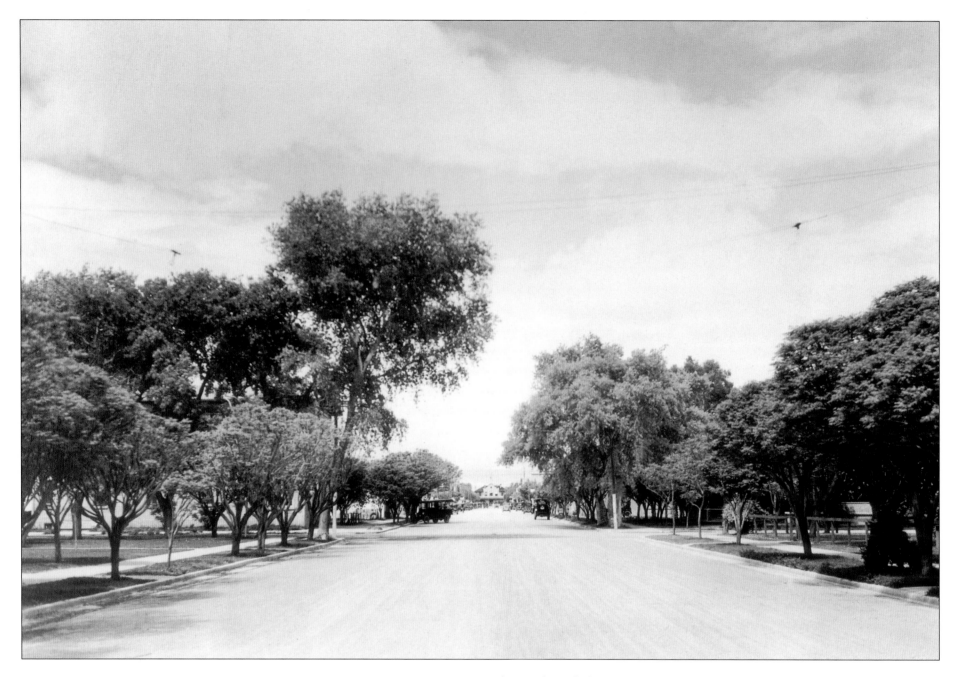

The residential character of Fremont Street is apparent in this view taken near the intersection of Fifth and Fremont in 1925. At this time, some of the town's most prominent pioneer families, such as the Parks and the Squires, made their homes here. Commercial development in the 1930s and 1940s forced many to relocate to other parts of town.

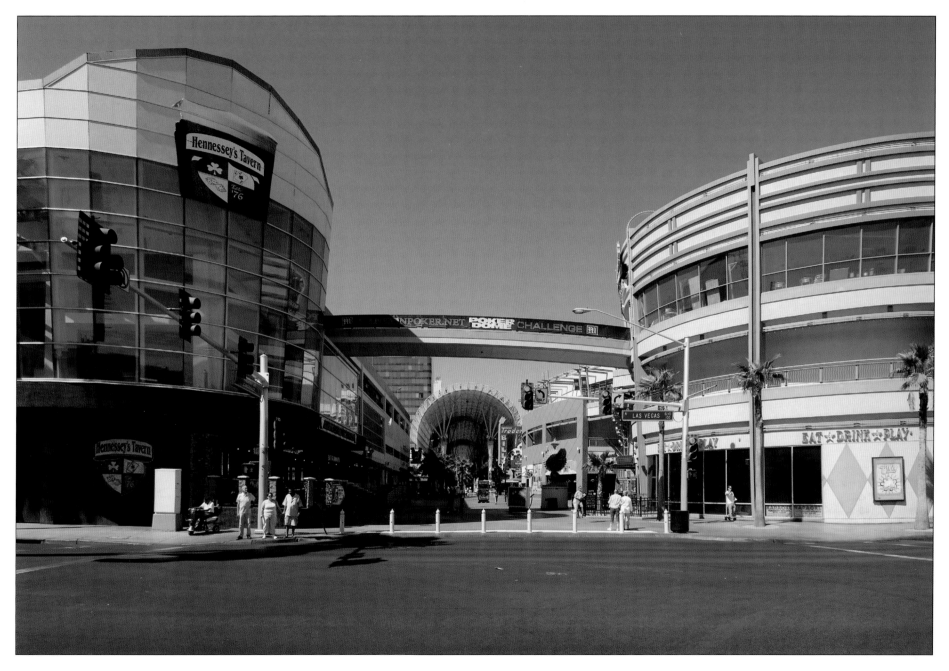

Fifth Street, now an extension of Las Vegas Boulevard, marks the eastern boundary of the five-block Fremont Street Experience. The houses and shade trees disappeared long ago, and in their place is the Neonopolis complex to the right. At its May 2002 opening, city officials were optimistic that the open-air shopping, food, and entertainment complex, decorated with antique neon signs, would aid in the revitalization of downtown Las Vegas. Whether or not the Neonopolis contributed to downtown revitalization is a point of debate between some. But indeed, rumors that downtown is ripe for renaissance have many proponents. Once merely an afterthought for tourists seeking the spectacle of the Strip, it is today of interest to both visitors and imaginative real-estate developers.

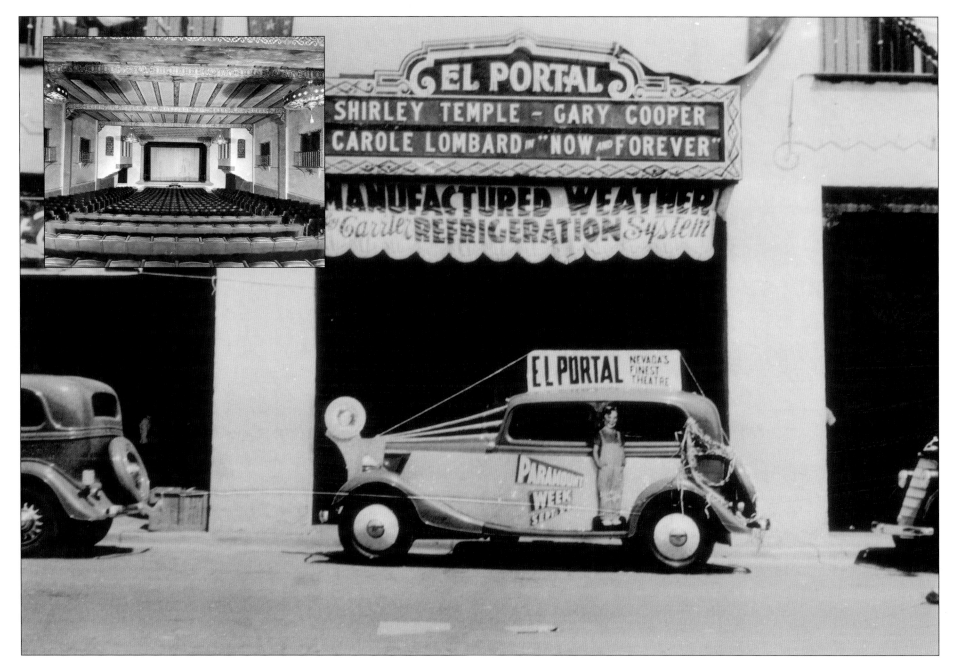

The El Portal theater at 310 Fremont opened on June 21, 1928, with a prerelease screening of Clara Bow's film *Ladies of the Mob*. With its organ loft and orchestra pit, the theater also served as a venue for plays, music recitals, and vaudeville shows. It was one of the first buildings in Las Vegas to install air-conditioning—a feature its owners were eager to promote, as this photo from the mid-1930s demonstrates. The inset shows the interior of the El Portal, which was decorated in a Spanish motif and featured a lobby bordered in colored tiles. Hand-painted ceiling beams and chandeliers completed the elegant interior, which had a seating capacity of 713, including eighty-four cushioned high-back loge chairs.

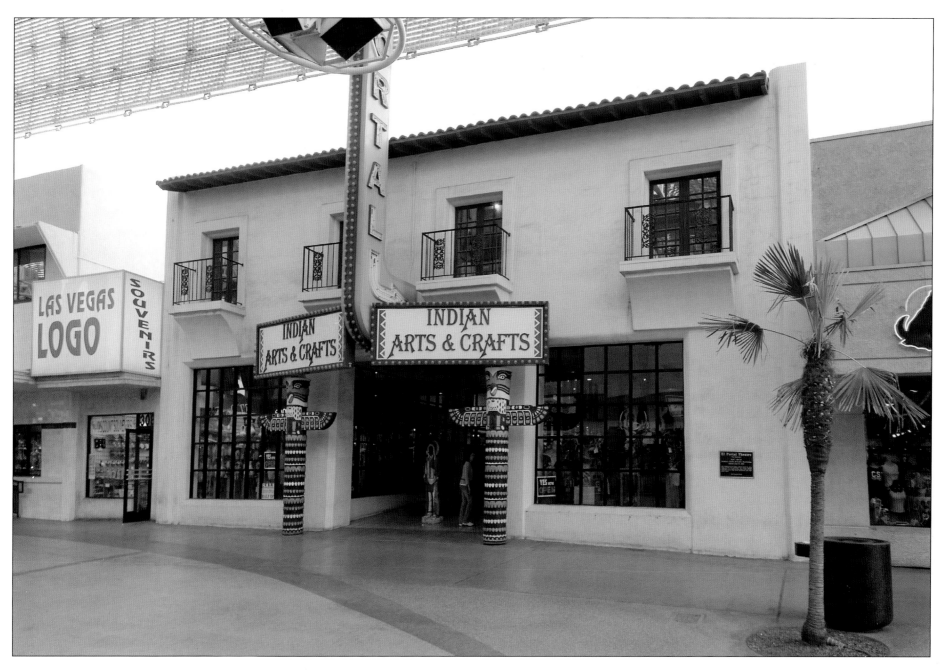

By the late 1950s, the tiny El Portal struggled to compete with the larger
theater venues in Las Vegas. After the theater closed in the late 1970s, the
building became home to El Portal Gifts. Today it houses the Indian Arts
& Crafts store. Traces of its glory days remain in the original neon sign that
decorates the front, and in the heavy wood ceiling beams that decorate the
store's interior.

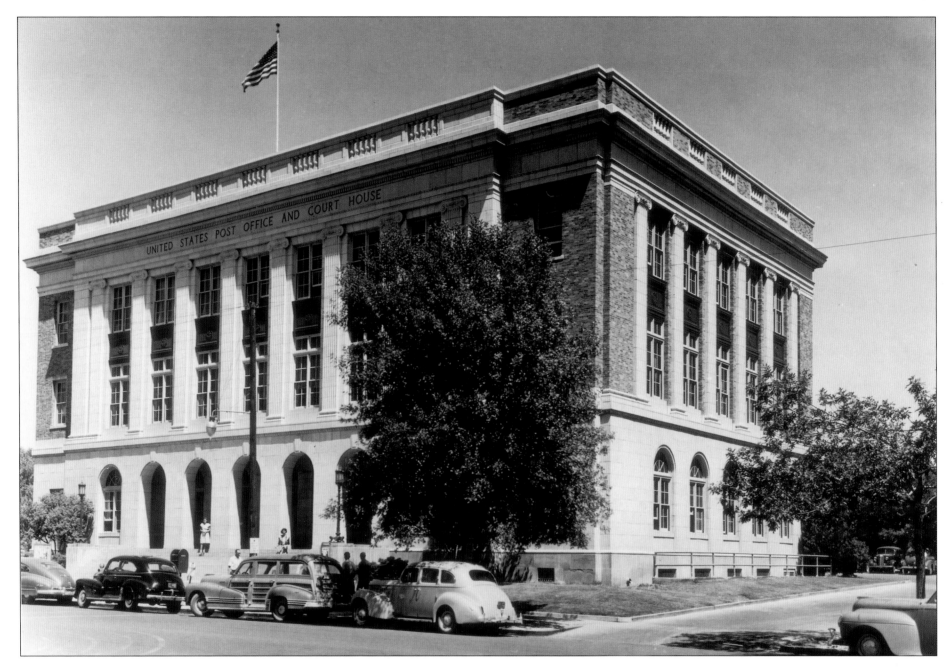

The United States Post Office and Court House on 301 East Stewart Avenue near Third was completed in 1933, and is shown here in the late 1940s. The neoclassical structure with its sturdy brick exterior was constructed as part of an extensive federal government building program begun in the late 1920s by the Hoover administration—a forerunner of Franklin D. Roosevelt's Public Works Administration program.

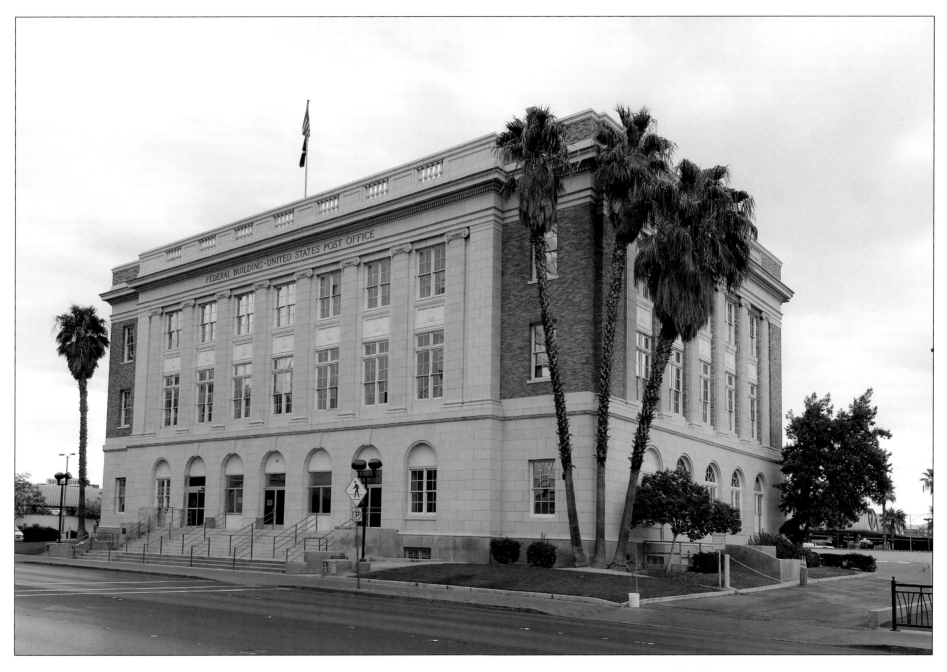

Entered on the National Register of Historic Places in February 1983, the United States Post Office and Court House currently contains offices for the U.S. Tax Court, Social Security Administration, and Postal Service. In April 2002, the City of Las Vegas took possession of the historic structure with plans to turn it into a museum or educational facility. In 2003, the city contracted an architectural firm to analyze the feasibility of such a cultural center, appropriately enough dubbed the POST Modern. Since then, much attention has been given to the rules and regulations of properly executing such a renovation while preserving the historical property. It's bound to succeed. As Roosevelt was fond of saying, "Far and away the best prize that life offers is the chance to work hard at work worth doing."

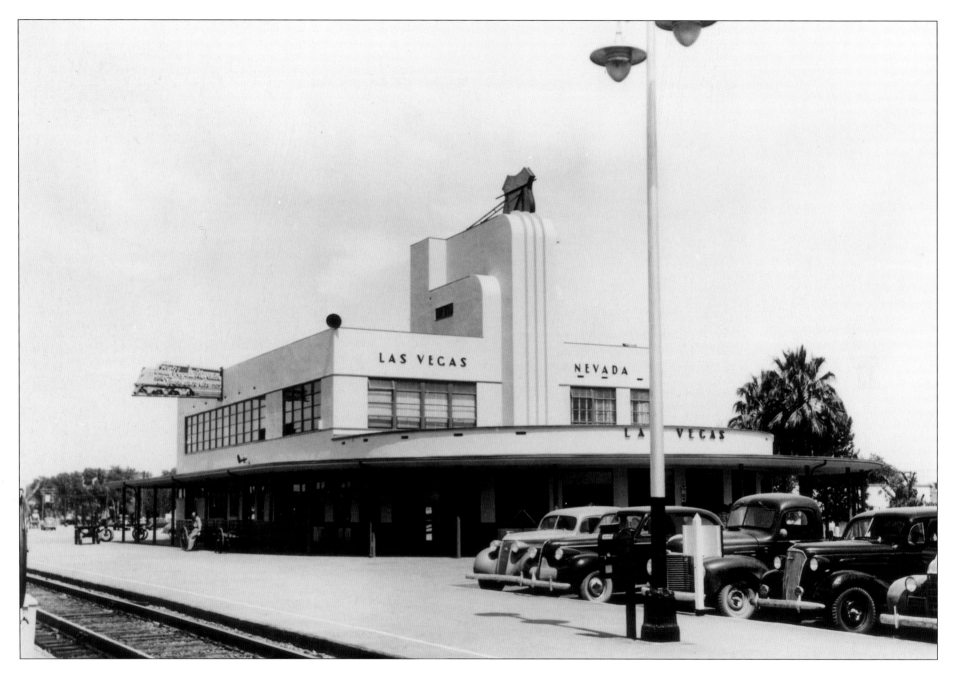

In 1940, the gleaming new Union Pacific railroad station took the place of the original Mission-style Salt Lake Depot at Main and Fremont. Contemporary publicity described its style as the "typical modernistic Western motif" and billed the Union Pacific Station as "the first streamlined, completely air-conditioned railroad passenger station anywhere."

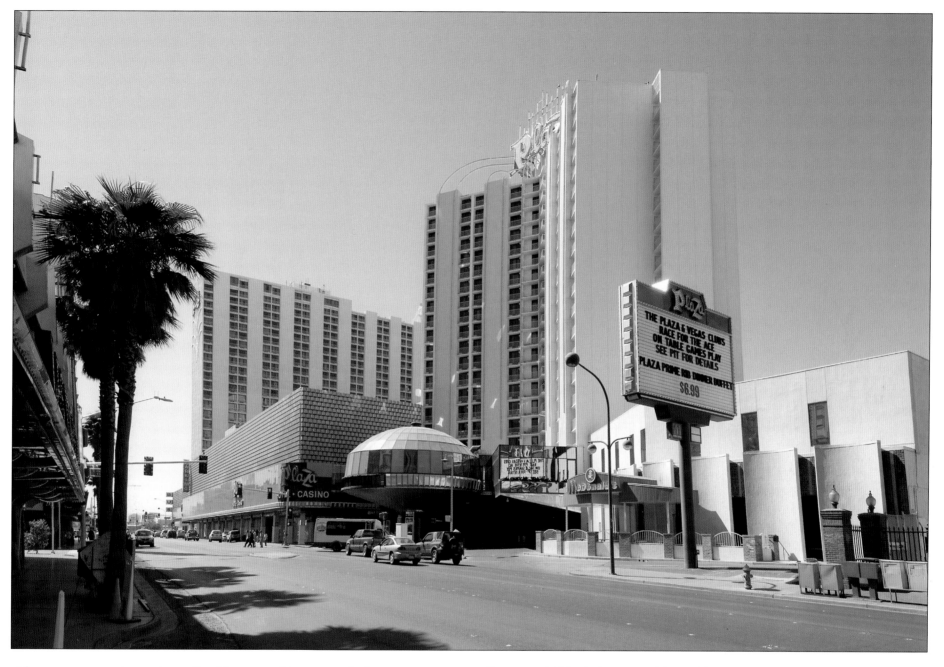

After passenger train service to Las Vegas was discontinued, the twenty-six-story Union Plaza Hotel was constructed just in front of the original Union Pacific Station as a joint venture between the Union Pacific Railroad and a private corporation. The hotel opened on July 2, 1971, with what was then the world's largest casino. One of four properties owned by downtown casino mogul Jackie Gaughan, it was renamed Jackie Gaughan's Plaza Hotel and

Casino in 1992. As he entered his golden years, Gaughan turned the daily operations of his casinos over to his son, Michael Gaughan. Today, Jackie Gaughan is known as a Las Vegas legend whose many interests and eye for business execution have left his fingerprints on some of the most interesting deals and decades of the city's history.

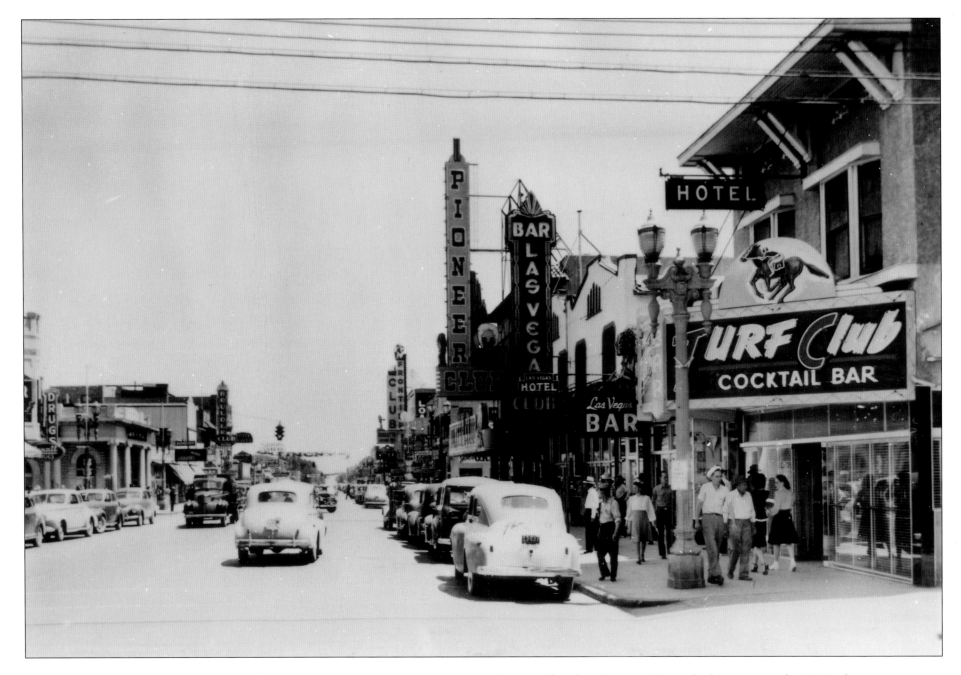

A view of bustling Fremont Street looking east in the 1940s shows a landscape of tightly clustered casinos, businesses, and neon signs. Although gambling establishments were dominant, Fremont Street also served as the town's main business district at the time, with businesses such as banks, drug stores, and liquor stores serving residents and visitors. With a political banner stretched across the street, downtown Las Vegas looks like a typical 1940s American city.

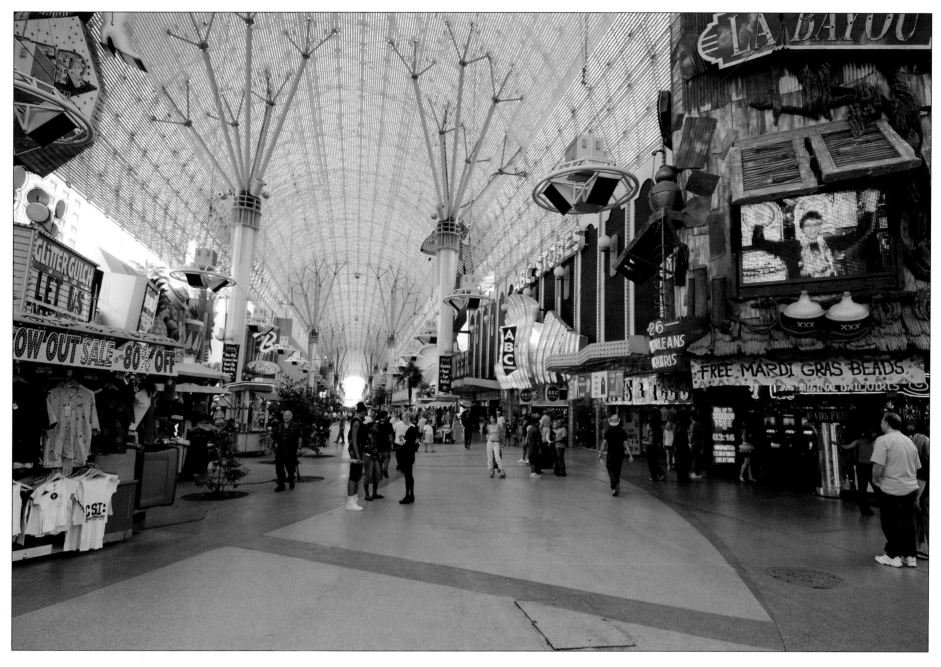

Fremont Street looks like anything but a typical American city today. No longer the town's main business thoroughfare, it is a pedestrian mall designed to entice tourists to visit downtown Las Vegas. Casinos still line the street, but souvenir shops and gift kiosks have taken the place of other businesses; the Pioneer is now strictly a gift shop. Today's Fremont Street has a patina of commercial engineering and an air of tourist chic wholly absent in the Fremont Street of old. One is now more likely to meet the spouse of a Nebraska conventioneer than someone in the railroad or cattle industry.

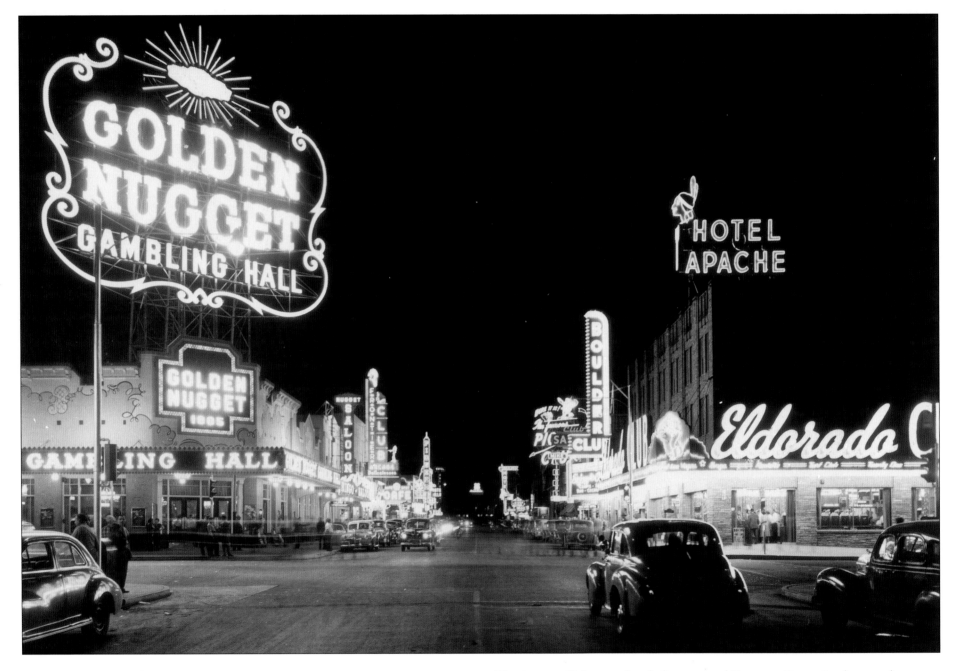

Classic neon lights up the skyline around Fremont Street in the area known as "Glitter Gulch" in 1950. The spectacular open-frame neon sign atop the Golden Nugget, some forty-eight feet high and forty-eight feet wide, was designed by Hermon Boernge of the Young Electric Sign Company. The "gold nugget" at the top of the sign was twelve feet wide and its neon rays spread some twenty-six feet.

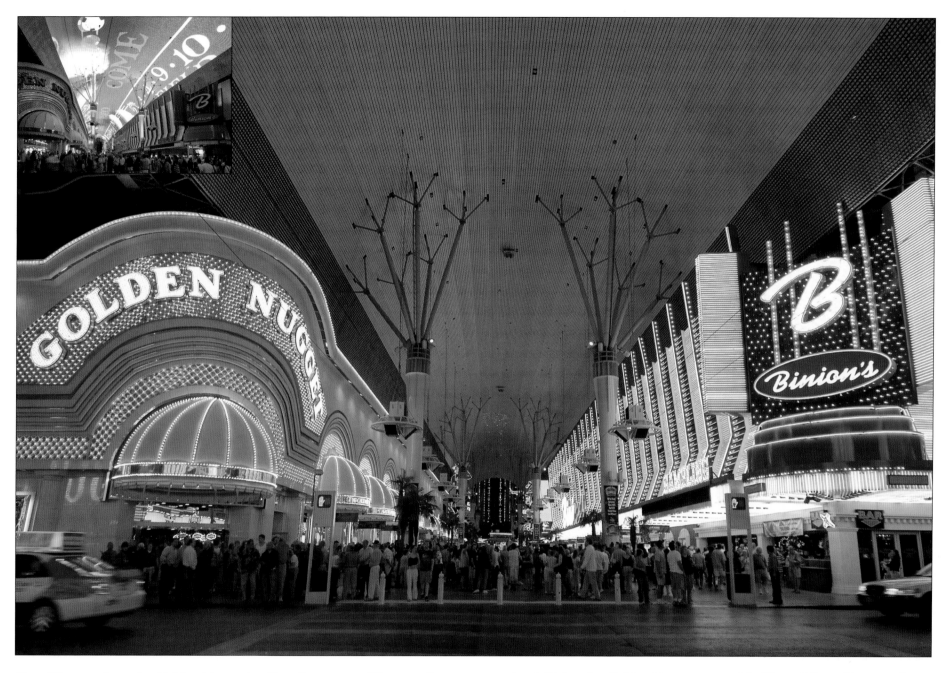

Over fifty years later, the Golden Nugget is still a vibrant part of Fremont Street but was transformed into an elegant resort by Steve Wynn in the mid-1980s. In an area where neon reigns supreme, the restrained gold and white exterior makes its own statement. It contrasts sharply with the vibrant blue and gold neon of Binion's Horseshoe, which replaced the Eldorado Club in 1951. Crowds gather every hour from dusk to midnight to watch a spectacular light show overhead. Today, the Golden Nugget is owned by Texan Tilman Fertitta, who performed a major corporate restructuring in 2006 in an effort to reposition the casino's marketing strategy. A renovation of the sixty-year-old classic casino is on the horizon. Fertitta, the president and CEO of Landry's Restaurants Inc., is sure to bring excitement to his administration of the Nugget.

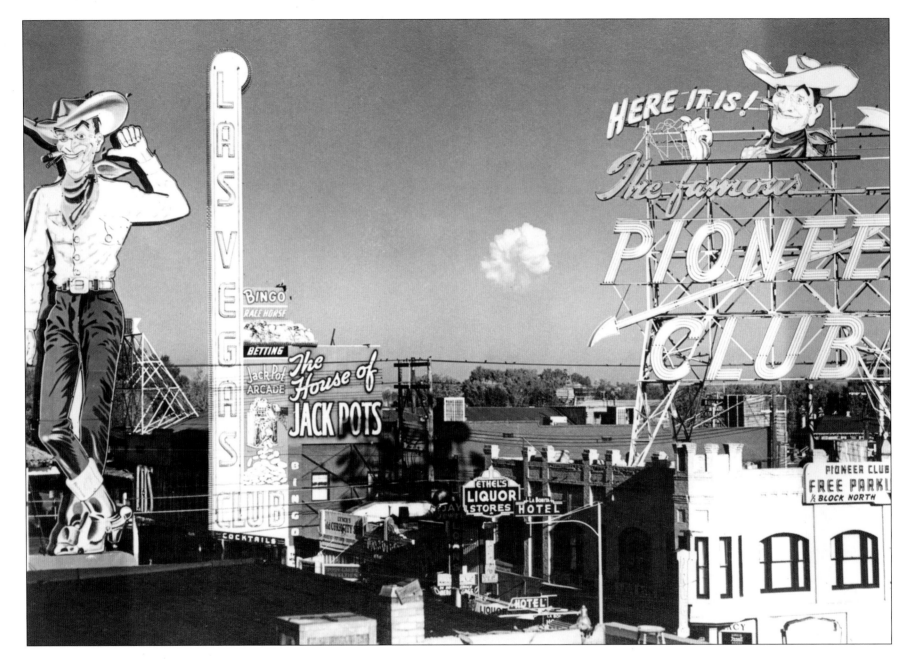

A white mushroom cloud from the nearby Nevada Test Site overshadows Vegas Vic, symbol of Las Vegas hospitality, in this famous photo taken April 18, 1953. Established by the U.S. government in 1951, the Nevada Test Site was located in a barren desert area just northwest of Las Vegas. Most residents were blissfully unaware of the dangers posed by atomic testing, and the town promoted the blasts as just another Las Vegas tourist attraction.

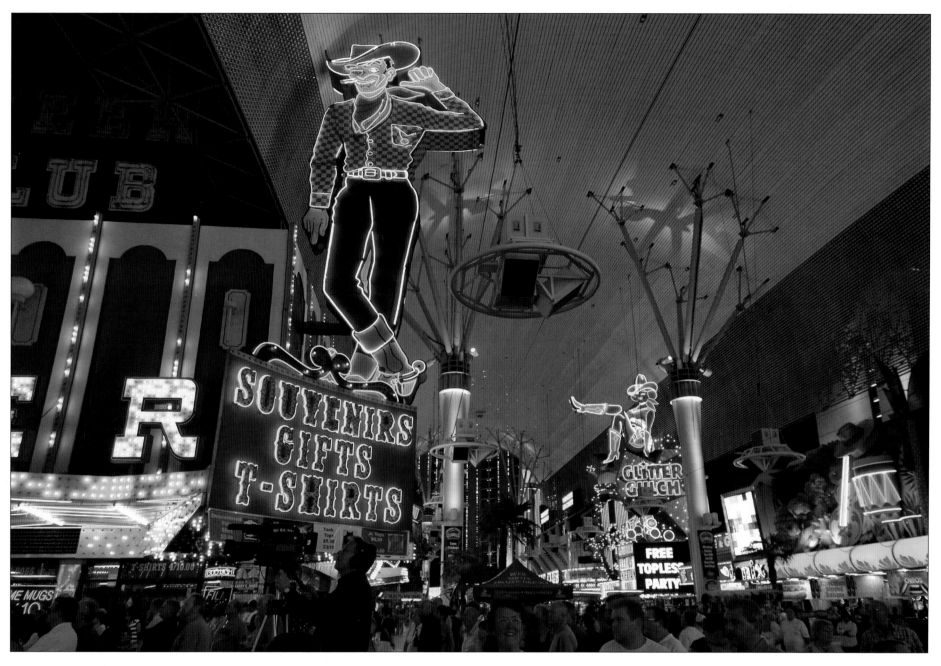

For decades, the famous forty-foot-tall neon cowboy waved his mechanical arm, boomed a friendly "Howdy, partner" to passersby, and generated smoke rings from his cigarette. Today the Glitter Gulch icon still greets tourists and locals alike, but he was silenced during the shooting of a Lee Marvin movie in 1966. A quarter-century later, his arm gave out. Now quiet, motionless, and a few feet shorter (to make room for the Fremont Street Experience), Vegas Vic still persists in pointing visitors toward the Pioneer Club. Proposals have been made by various private and public enterprises to help restore his various maladies but no true support outside of the emotional has surfaced. Topped by the monstrous Experience canopy, he's starting to look like just another neon sign despite his fame.

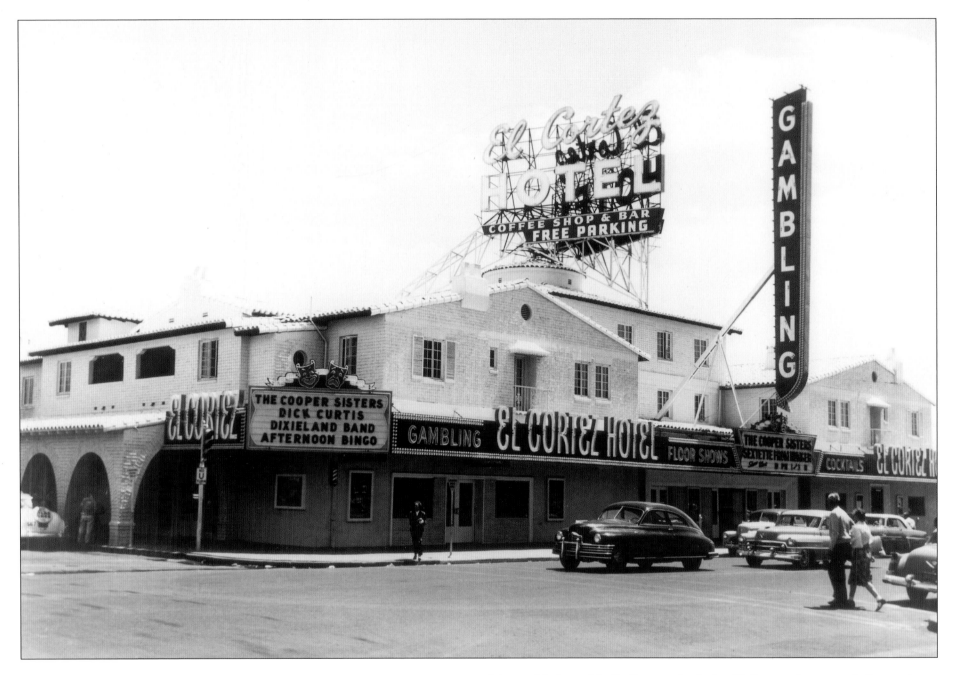

Marion Hicks and J. C. Grayson built the El Cortez, downtown's first major resort, for $245,000 in 1941. Critics felt the hotel's location at Sixth and Fremont was too far from downtown to make a profit, but it was apparently profitable enough to attract the attention of certain mob figures looking to buy a casino. For a brief period in 1945, the El Cortez counted among its owners Benjamin "Bugsy" Siegel, Meyer Lansky, Gus Greenbaum, Moe Sedway, Davie Berman, and Willie Alderman.

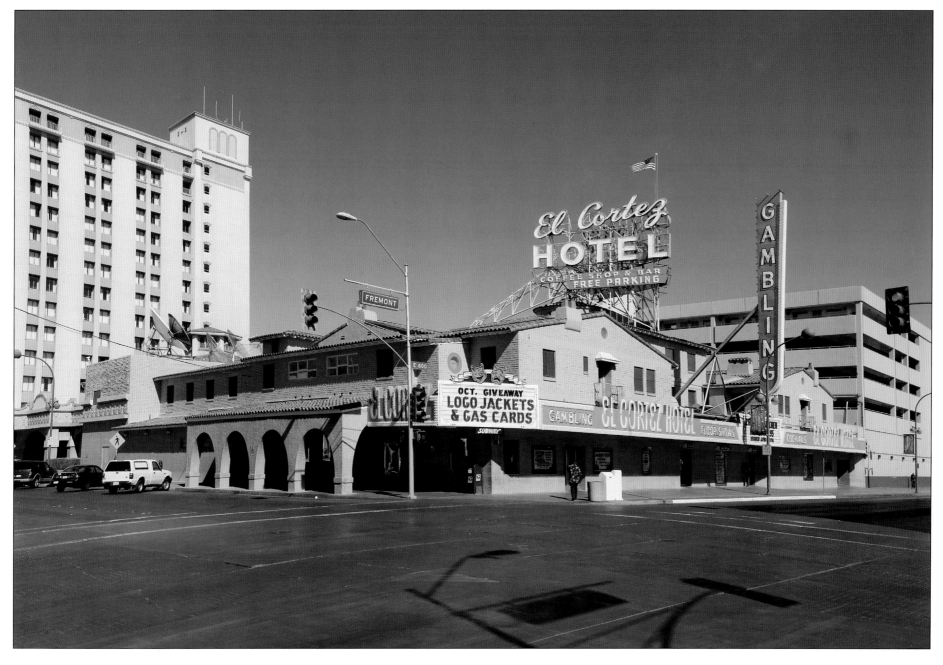

One of the only downtown buildings to retain its original facade, the El Cortez looks much the same as it did over sixty years ago. Aside from the satellite dishes on the roof and a few bars on the windows, the addition of an adjacent high-rise is the biggest change to the hotel's exterior. Including its neighboring tower, the hotel boasts a 300-room capacity. A part of the Jackie Gaughan legacy, the building recently underwent a renovation, beautifying the building and amenities without sacrificing its old-time Las Vegas look and feel. Despite its age, it remains popular with locals and visitors seeking a good bargain and a possible win betting on their $1 craps and 25-cent roulette.

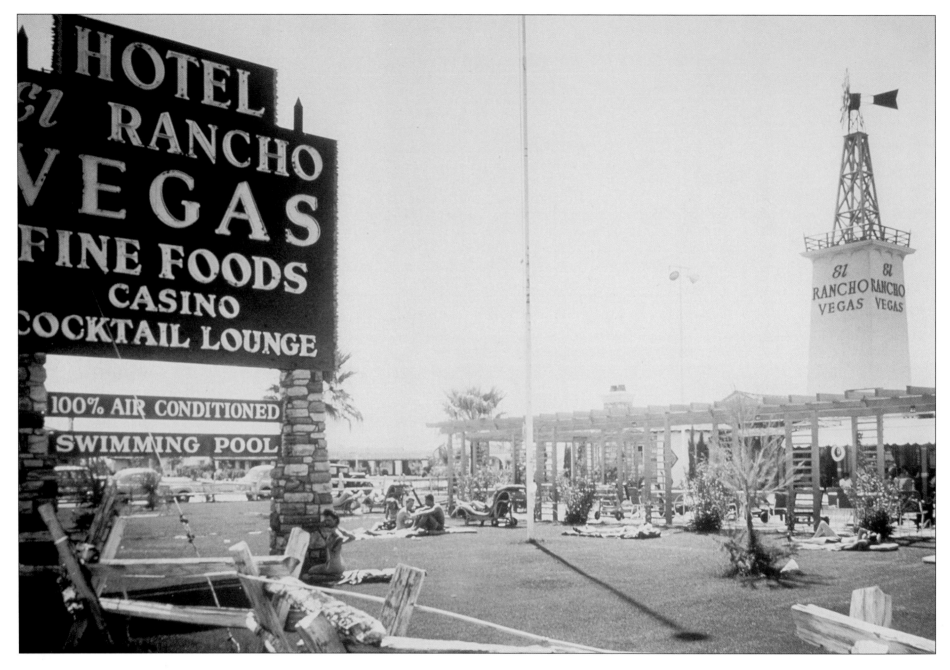

Highway 91 was just an empty stretch of road leading into Las Vegas when California hotelier Thomas Hull, attracted by lower land and tax costs, decided to build a hotel at its intersection with San Francisco (now Sahara) Avenue. His El Rancho Vegas, with its trademark windmill accenting a ranchlike Spanish mission design, opened on April 3, 1941. It was the first resort hotel to open on what would soon be known as the Las Vegas Strip.

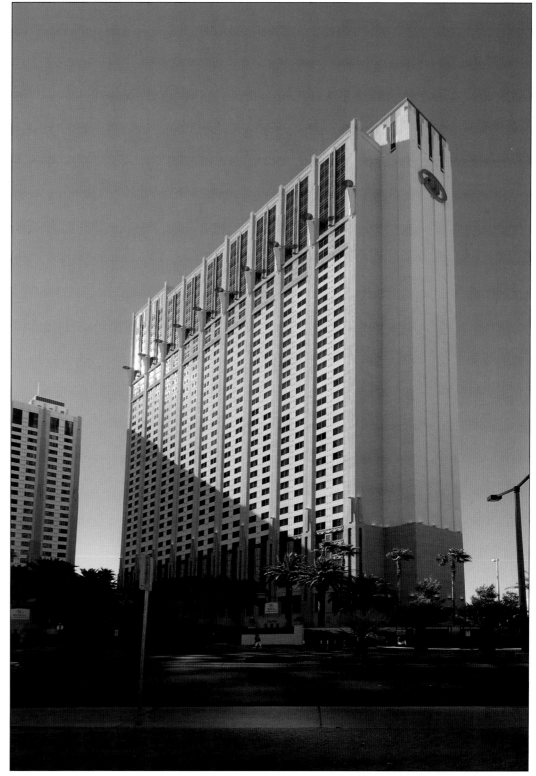

In 1960, the El Rancho Vegas was destroyed in a suspicious fire. Although owner Beldon Katleman announced plans to rebuild the hotel, the promised resort never materialized. The lot remained vacant for years. Howard Hughes bought the land in 1970 and at one point casino owner Bob Stupak even considered developing a *Titanic*-themed property. But the projects fell through. In 2001, construction began on a time-share resort in a ten-acre area at the south end of the site. In November 2003, Vegas's third Hilton Grand Vacation Club opened the doors of its 540-unit, twenty-seven-story tower, the first in a series of four on the site. A second thirty-eight-story tower went up in 2006. The rest of the site is titled to Sahara owner William Bennett, who may one day construct a new casino-resort on the lot. In the meantime, hundreds of tourists stroll by the site daily as they make their way down Las Vegas Boulevard, most of them unaware of its historic founding role in the development of the Strip.

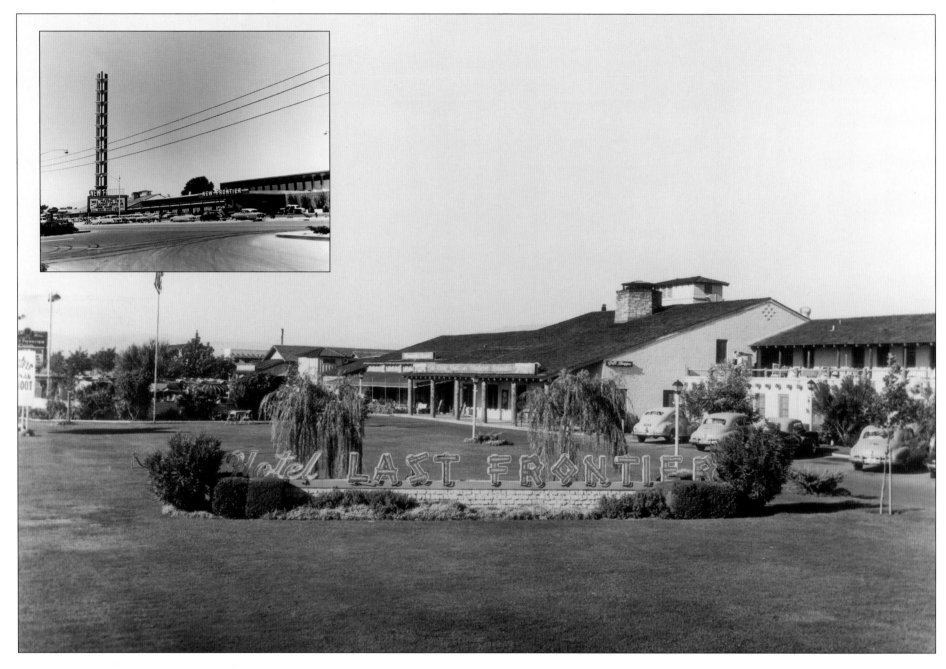

Main: "The Early West in Modern Splendor" was the theme of the Last Frontier Hotel, which opened on October 30, 1942. The second major resort on the Strip sported headboards that resembled oxen yoke and featured the old Arizona Club's famous mahogany bar. To the north of the main complex was the Last Frontier Village, a re-creation of a frontier town complete with its own wedding chapel known as the Little Church of the West.

Inset: The Last Frontier was sold in 1951, and again in 1955. Its new owners would dramatically change the hotel to reflect their theme: "The New Frontier: Out of This World." The old west decor was replaced with a space-age, ultramodern design that featured an interior done in chrome and aluminum and accented with reds, blues, and purples. Its Cloud 9 bar was thought to be the world's longest at the time.

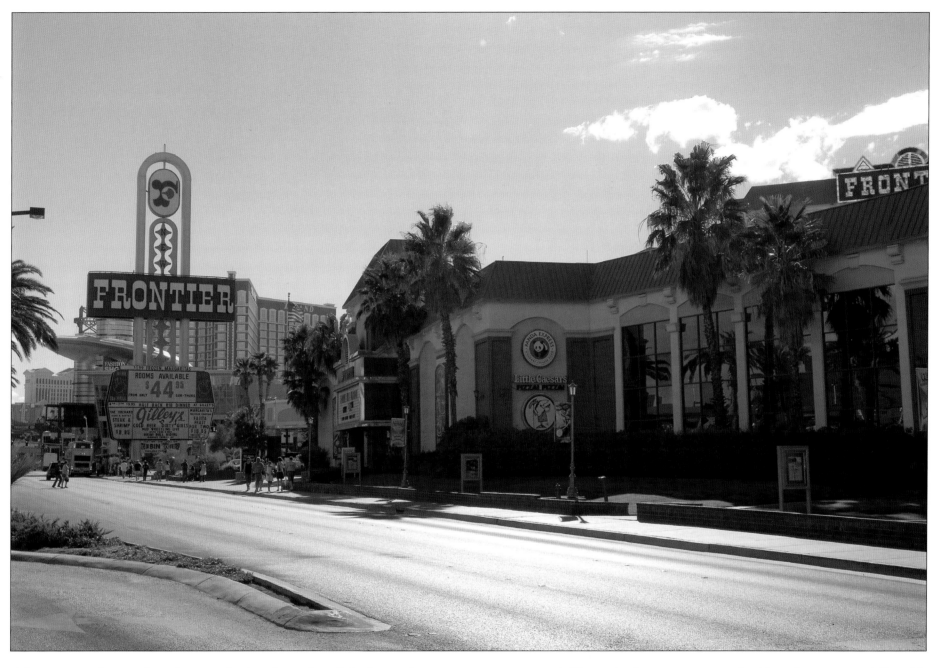

After a series of ownership changes, the hotel was demolished to make way for a new building that opened in July 1967. Howard Hughes purchased the property soon afterward and shortened its name to the Frontier. In 1988, the hotel was sold to the Elardi family and became the site of a bitter union strike that lasted over six years until the hotel was sold to Phil Ruffin in October 1997. It was rechristened the New Frontier in 1999. From 2000 on, plans to implode the New Frontier to make room for another megaresort were rumored. The casino's owners partnered with real estate mogul Donald Trump to build the Trump International Hotel & Tower, a high-rise luxury hotel-condominium, on some of the property. Since part of the original building still exists, some call the New Frontier the oldest Strip hotel and casino. Among the plans on the drawing board for the future: a 485-foot-high Ferris wheel similar to the London Eye in England.

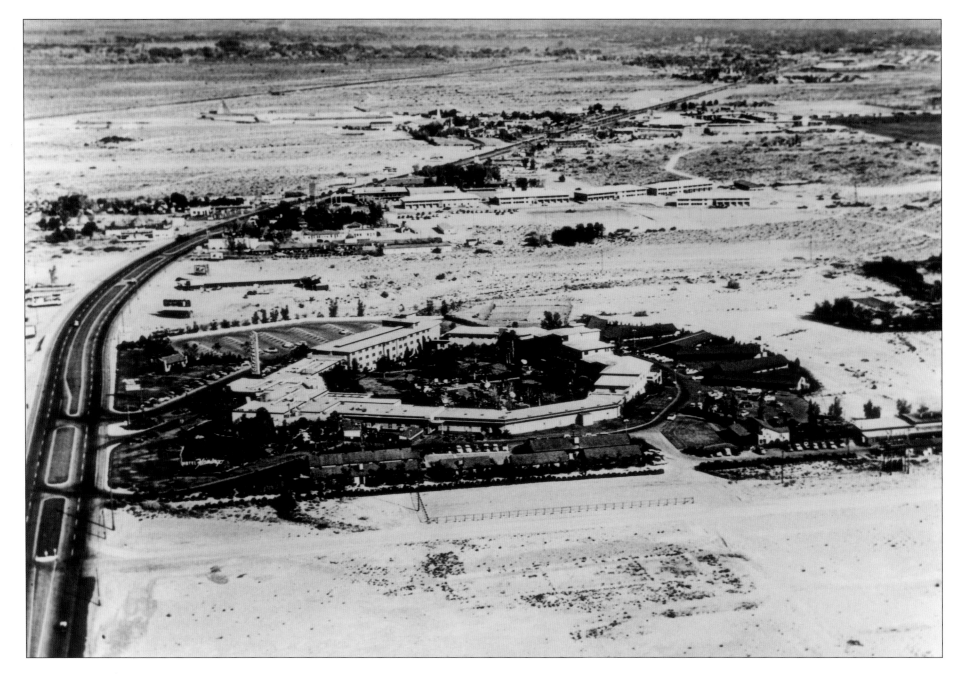

This shot shows the fabulous Flamingo as it looked in the early 1950s, when it was still bounded by desert. Although Southern California businessman Billy Wilkerson began construction on the resort, it was Benjamin "Bugsy" Siegel, using borrowed mob funds, who completed it at a cost that may have reached over $6 million. At its grand opening on December 26, 1946, only the casino, restaurant, and theater were complete—the hotel was finished in March 1947.

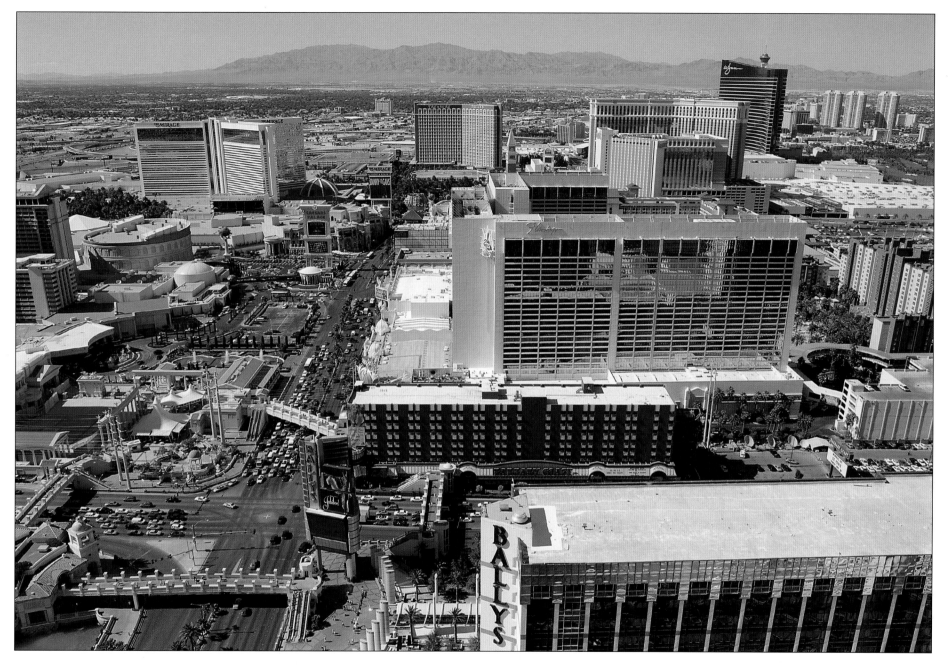

In July 1970, Kirk Kerkorian signed an agreement with Baron Hilton to purchase both the International (now the Las Vegas Hilton) and the Flamingo, which in 1971 officially became the Flamingo Hilton. Its original bungalows have been replaced by a series of high-rise towers, and landscaping no longer envelops the hotel but is confined to the space between the towers. The last vestige of the old Flamingo constructed by Siegel was bulldozed in 1993. In 1994, Hilton constructed two $104 million, 612-room Art Deco towers containing 201 suite time-shares. The Hilton Grand Vacations was the first time-share on a major Strip hotel property and raised the Flamingo's total number of rooms and suites to 3,638. As part of a $130 million renovation and expansion, the Flamingo Hilton (now owned by Harrah's Entertainment) includes a Caribbean-style water playground and wildlife habitat complete with penguins, swans, turtles, and—sure enough—a flock of live Chilean flamingos.

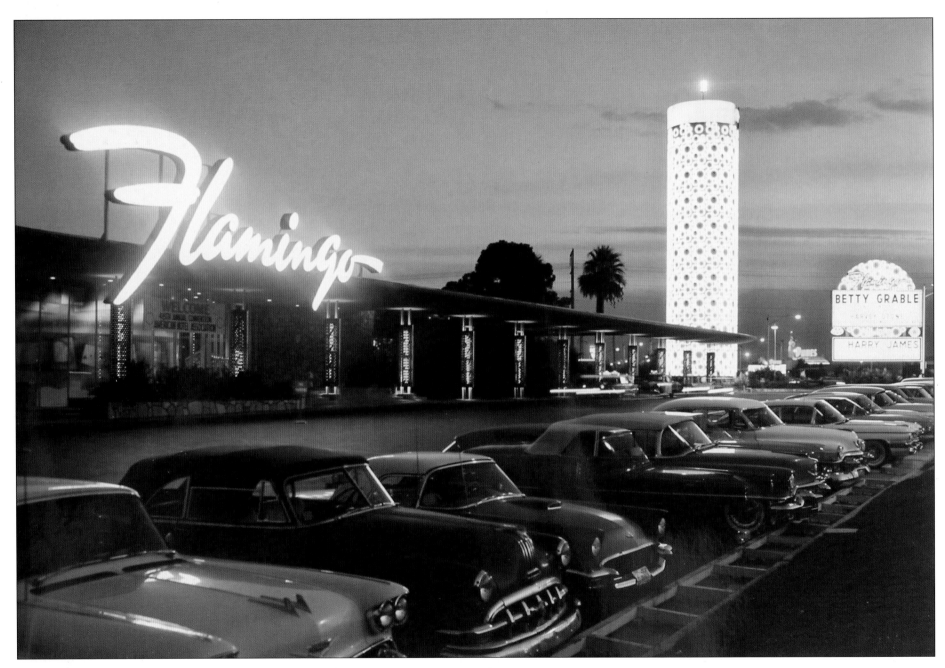

In 1953, the Flamingo installed this spectacular eighty-foot "Champagne Tower" with glowing neon rings in front of the hotel. A Las Vegas landmark for years, it was the tallest freestanding sign structure on the Strip during the 1950s. It was demolished in 1968 after Kirk Kerkorian bought the property and made extensive renovations that completely changed the look of the hotel.

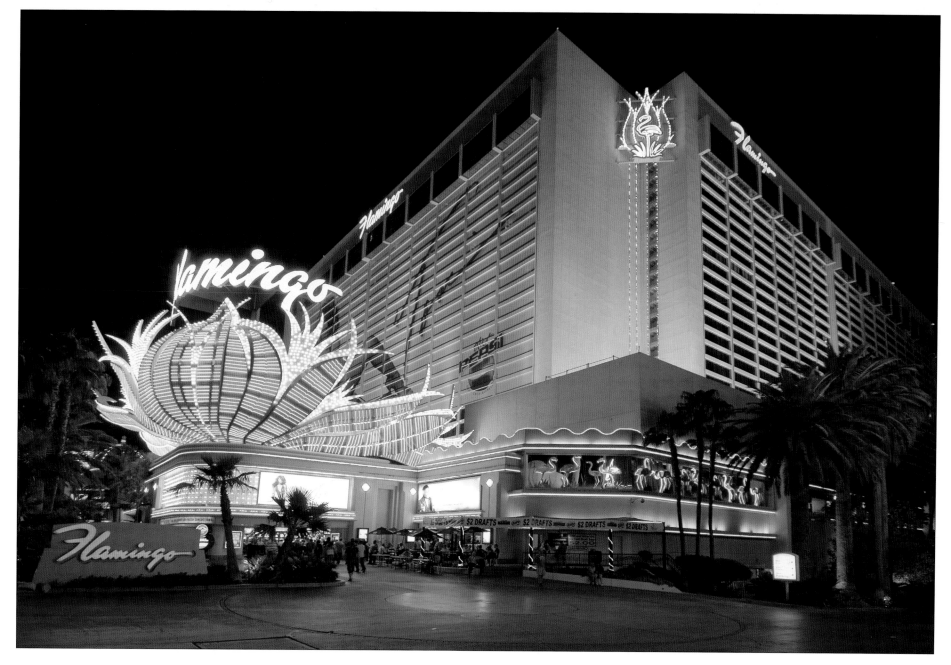

The hotel with one of the most colorful pasts in Las Vegas is fittingly adorned with some of the most spectacular neon on the Strip. Designed by Paul Rodriquez and installed in 1976, the neon features swirling fuchsia and orange feathers surrounded by a band of neon-illuminated flamingos. They cast a warm glow on one of the Strip's busiest intersections and have become synonymous with Las Vegas, probably used more than any other icon in movies and television as an establishing shot for the glitzy city. And its inside is equally ritzy, complete with spa, fitness center, tennis courts, eight restaurants ranging from the exotic to the casual, three different bars, and its own exclusive golf course. In 2006, the Flamingo featured the legendary Second City comedy improv troupe.

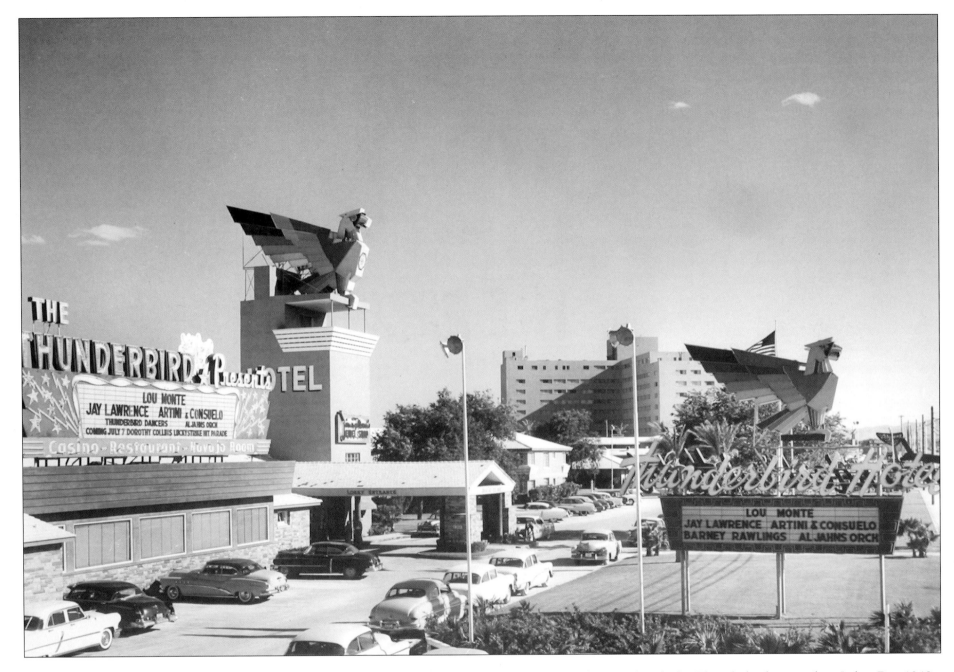

The Strip's fourth major hotel, the Thunderbird, opened on Labor Day 1948. The Indian-themed resort with its trademark neon bird took its name from a Navajo legend. In 1955, it became the first hotel to have its gaming license suspended after allegations surfaced that its owners had failed to report investments made by underworld figures. After a period of litigation, the Nevada Supreme Court ruled in favor of the Thunderbird.

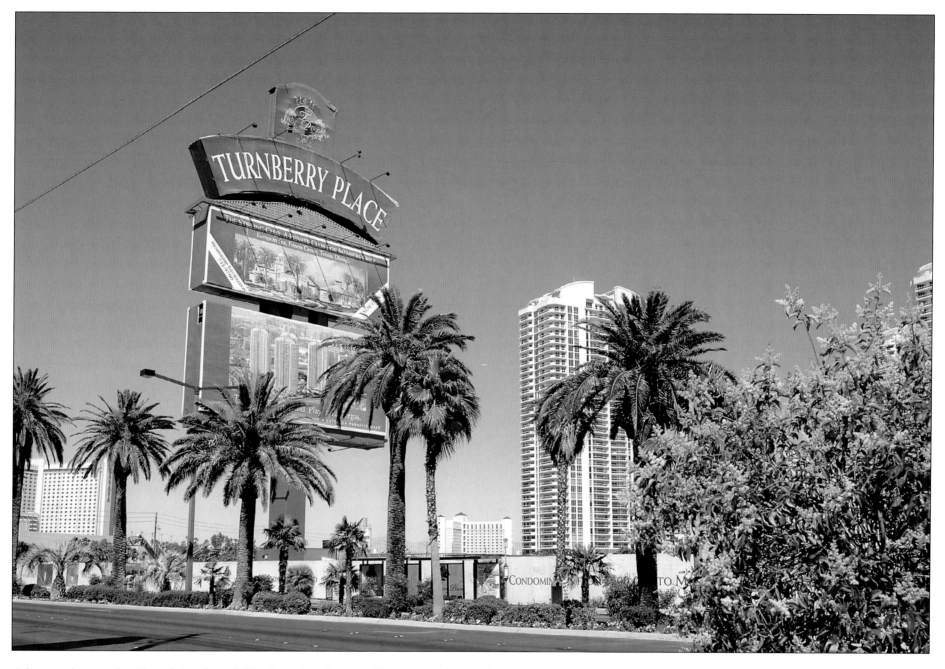

After purchasing the Thunderbird in 1977, Major Arteburn Riddle reopened the hotel as the Silverbird. In 1982, new owners gave it a Southwest facade and renamed it the El Rancho (not to be confused with the Strip's original El Rancho). After its closure in 1992, the new El Rancho lay vacant until Turnberry Associates, developers of the upscale Turnberry Place condominium project, purchased the site in May 2000 with plans to develop a $700 million luxury high-rise community and casino. The El Rancho buildings were imploded in October 2000. They have been replaced by the four forty-story Turnberry Place towers. The fourth tower was completed in 2006. Just a block off the Strip and with an eye for blending upscale with anonymous, Turnberry Place has become one of the chicest new addresses in town.

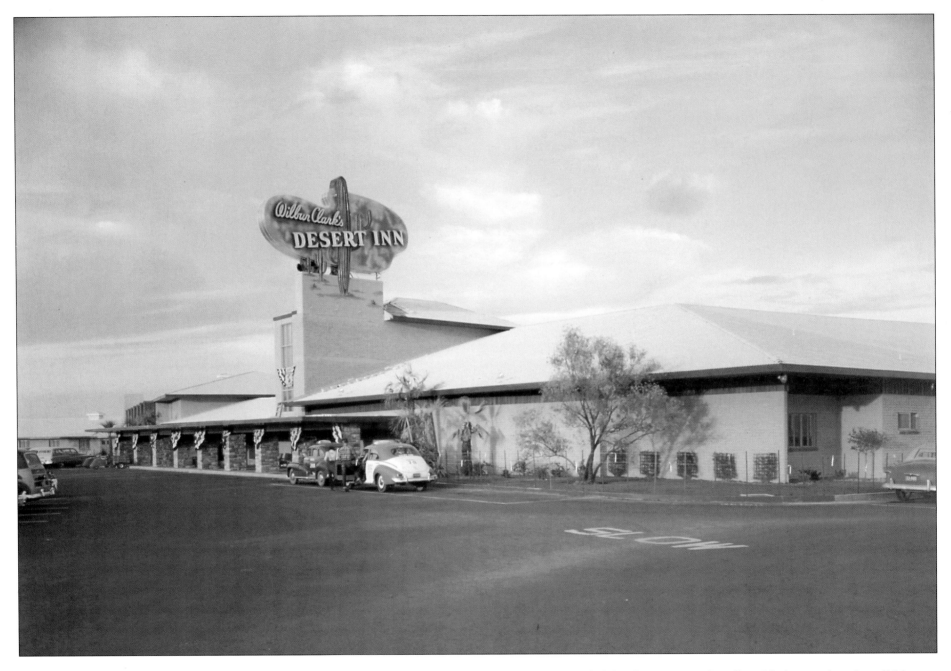

Moe Dalitz provided the financing and Wilbur Clark served as the affable public face for the Desert Inn, which opened on April 24, 1950. The hotel's trademark colors of Bermuda pink and bright green reflected its Southwest theme and complemented a unique roof composed of white tile chips. The Painted Desert Room featured world-class entertainers and the elegant Sky Room with its mountain views was a favorite with visitors.

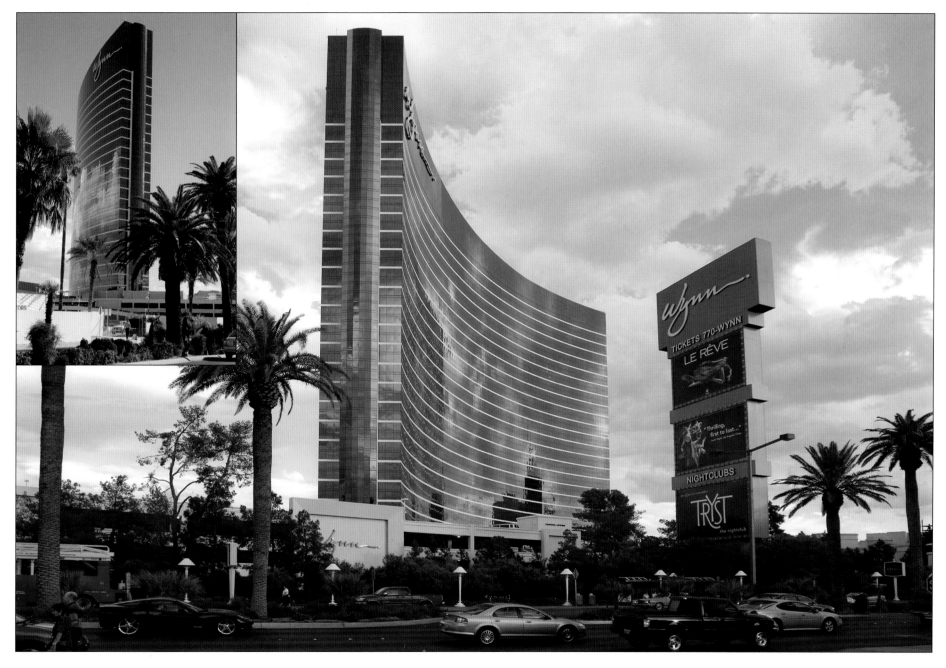

Soon after the property celebrated its fiftieth anniversary in 2000, Steve Wynn purchased the hotel for his wife's birthday. In 2001, Wynn announced plans to construct the megaresort Le Rêve on the former site of the Desert Inn. French for "the dream," Le Rêve was named after a Picasso masterpiece owned by Wynn and his wife, Elaine. Implosion of portions of the old Desert Inn took place in October 2001. On April 28, 2005, the $2.7 billion luxury hotel and destination casino-resort opened to the public under its new name, Wynn Las Vegas. Viewable from many Vegas vistas, the curved brown resort's finer features include 2,716 high-end guest rooms and suites, a 111,000-square-foot casino, a Ferrari and Maserati dealership, and an eighteen-hole golf course. And just so the moniker Le Rêve didn't say adieu altogether, it's now the name of the Wynn's flagship show, which resembles Cirque du Soleil.

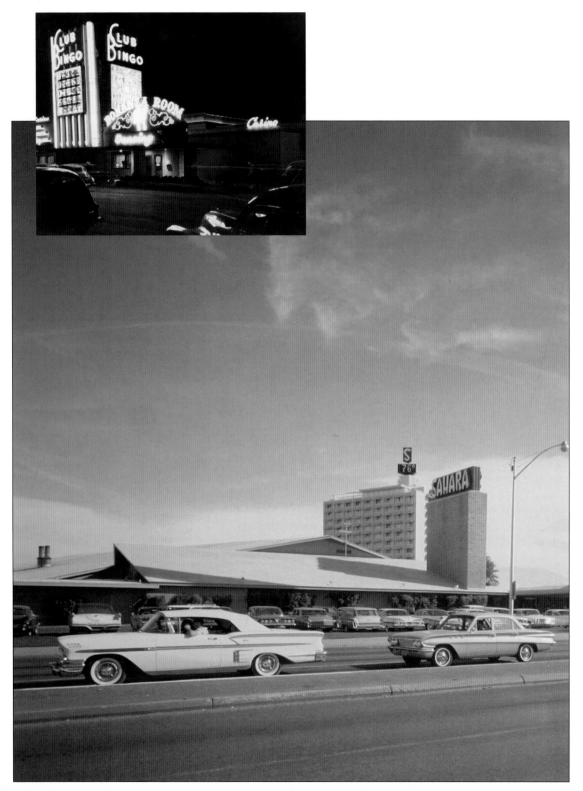

Inset: This is a night view of the Club Bingo, a 300-seat bingo parlor located at the corner of what was then San Francisco Street and Highway 91 (now Sahara and Las Vegas Boulevard), as it looked in the late 1940s.

Main: In October 1952, four years after its opening, owner Milton Prell enlarged and remodeled the Club Bingo into the African-themed Sahara Hotel. The fourteen-story tower shown here—the tallest structure in Nevada at the time—was added in 1966.

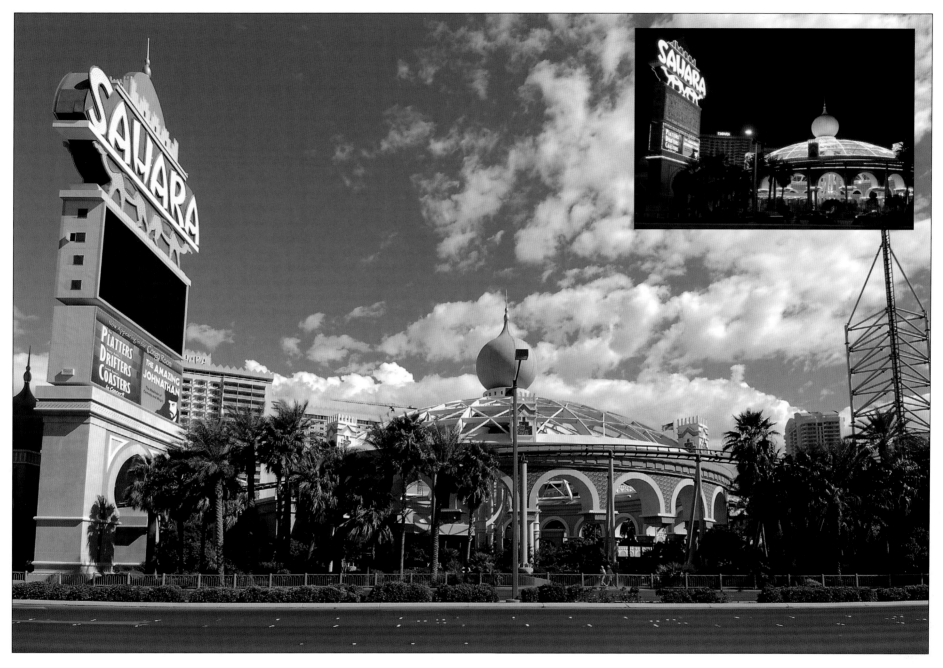

On October 7, 2002, the Sahara celebrated its fiftieth anniversary, becoming only the fourth original Strip property (after the Frontier, Flamingo, and Desert Inn) to achieve the golden milestone. Its exterior is dramatically different, however, as a result of a number of renovations and additions over the years. Its most recent renovation, completed in 1997, resulted in this Moroccan-themed structure with stylistic minarets and attractions such as the NASCAR Café and Speed roller coaster. Its tracks can be seen here encircling the hotel's exterior. The occasional speculation of a buying interest has been heard over the years, but the Sahara still packs in the crowds, not just for the gaming but also for shows such as the acclaimed comedy and magic of *The Amazing Jonathan*.

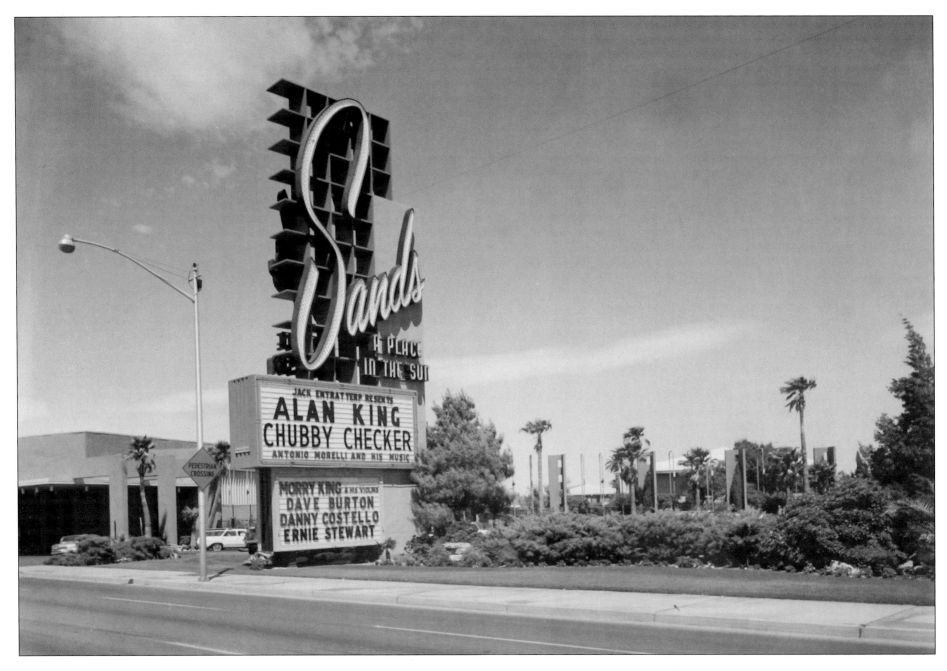

The hotel most closely associated with old-time Las Vegas glamour, the Sands, opened its doors on December 15, 1952. Designed in the Bermuda Modern style, the hotel's most popular attraction was the Copa Room, which featured beautiful showgirls and famous entertainers such as the Rat Pack. The distinctive sign and marquee of the Sands Hotel is shown here as it looked in 1964, just prior to the construction of the Sands Tower.

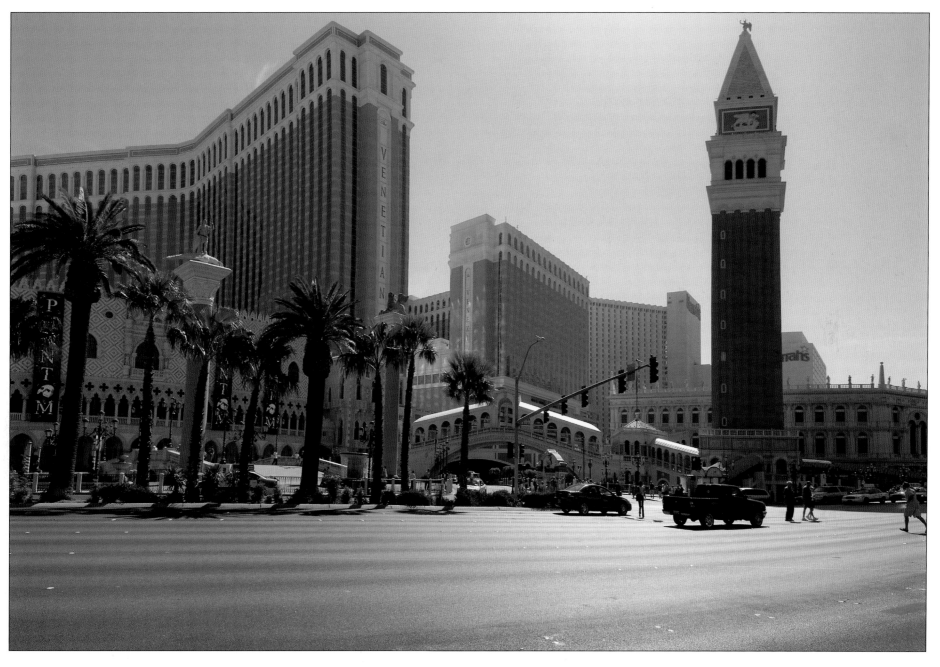

By 1996, the once-splendid Sands Hotel could no longer compete with the spectacle offered by the themed megaresorts that were proliferating throughout Las Vegas in the 1990s. The hotel and its famous tower were imploded in November 1996 to make way for the Venetian Resort-Hotel-Casino. The destruction of the hotel also provided Hollywood spectacle when footage of an airplane slamming into the soon-to-be destroyed casino was used in the film

Con Air. The Venetian is a major destination for fine dining, lavish suites, weddings, and—of course—its 120,000-square-foot casino. The facility has over 2,000 slot and video poker machines, poker, baccarat, blackjack, and single-O roulette, as well as a luxury horse racing and sports lounge. High-rollers find plenty of action here at semiprivate tables where hundreds of thousands of dollars change hands in a blink of the eye.

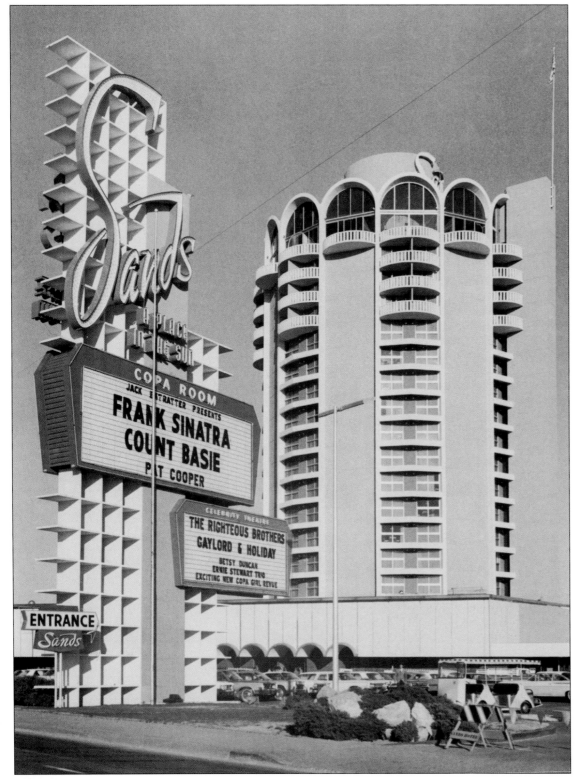

The Sands Hotel's trademark marquee is accented by the newly constructed seventeen-story Sands Tower in this 1966 photo. The tower, designed by noted architect Martin Stern, was part of a $9 million renovation completed in 1965. It was seen as a prototype for future Las Vegas high-rises and was widely copied. It was imploded on November 26, 1996, to make way for the Venetian Resort-Hotel-Casino.

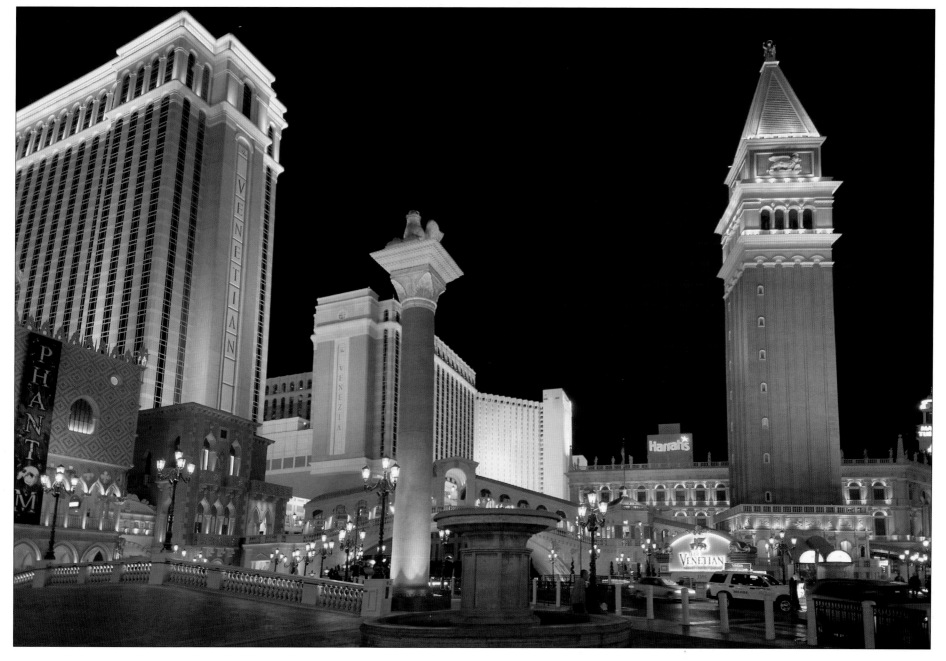

Constructed on the former site of the fabled Sands Hotel at a cost of $1.5 billion, the Venetian opened on May 3, 1999. With its cobbled walkways, replica of St. Mark's Square, and reproduction of Venice's Grand Canal, it has an "Old World" feel. And yet it boasts many modern amenities, including 4,000 luxury suites and an underground connection to the neighboring 1.2-million-square-foot Sands Convention Center. It's owned by a corporation that retains the Sands name and also owns the Sands Expo and Convention Center, as well as a Venetian resort in Macao and, soon, Singapore. The company scored a major innovation in vacation convenience when it successfully implemented airline baggage check-in at the hotel so guests could avoid waits at the airport. It was the first on the Strip to do so.

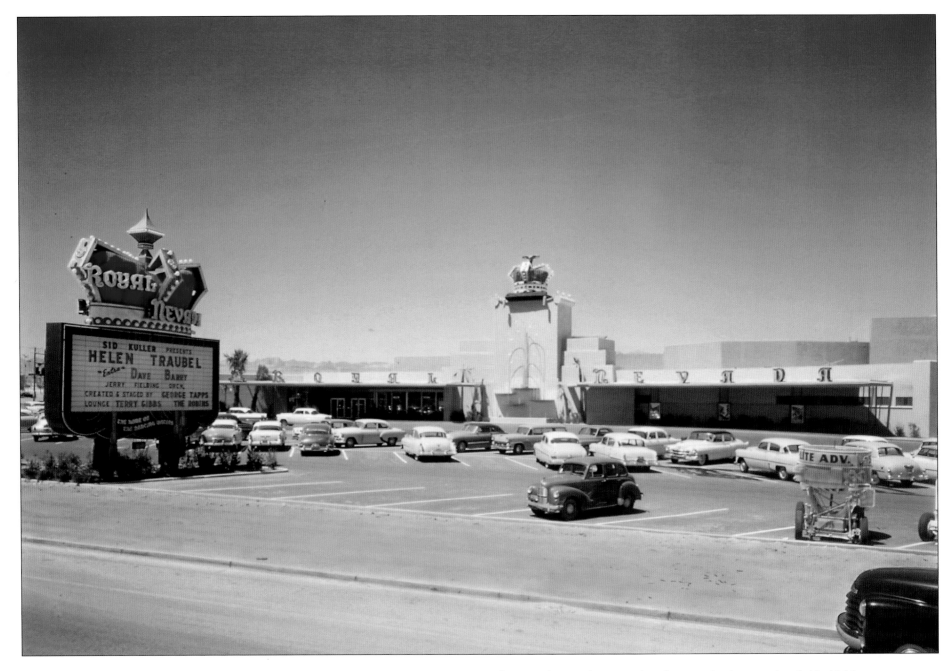

The Royal Nevada opened with great fanfare on April 19, 1955, just one day prior to the Riviera's opening. Located next to the New Frontier Hotel, the Royal Nevada was billed as the "Showplace of Showtown U.S.A." and featured opera singer Helen Traubel on its opening night. The hotel was also "Home of the Dancing Waters," an indoor fountain display composed of thirty-eight tons of cascading water that was accompanied by colorful lights and music.

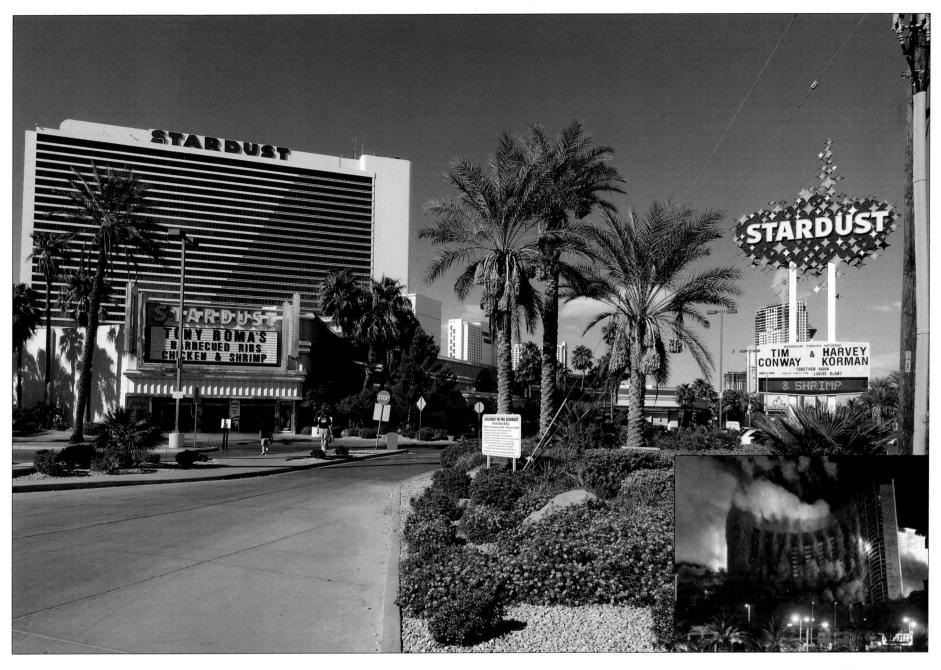

Despite its early promise, the Royal Nevada was plagued with financial problems from the start. Overbuilding on the Strip and a national economic recession resulted in troubles for all of the casinos that opened in spring 1955, but only the Royal Nevada completely disappeared. In 1959, it was absorbed into the south end of the Stardust Hotel. The Stardust fared better, but only just. In 2006, the casino ceased operation as fans of old Las Vegas hurried to see the place before it was demolished in March 2007 (see inset). Its owner, Boyd Gaming Corporation, is making way for its planned $4 billion Echelon Place project. Echelon Place will include 2,600 rooms, 700 suites, a 140,000-square-foot casino, and twenty-five restaurants and bars.

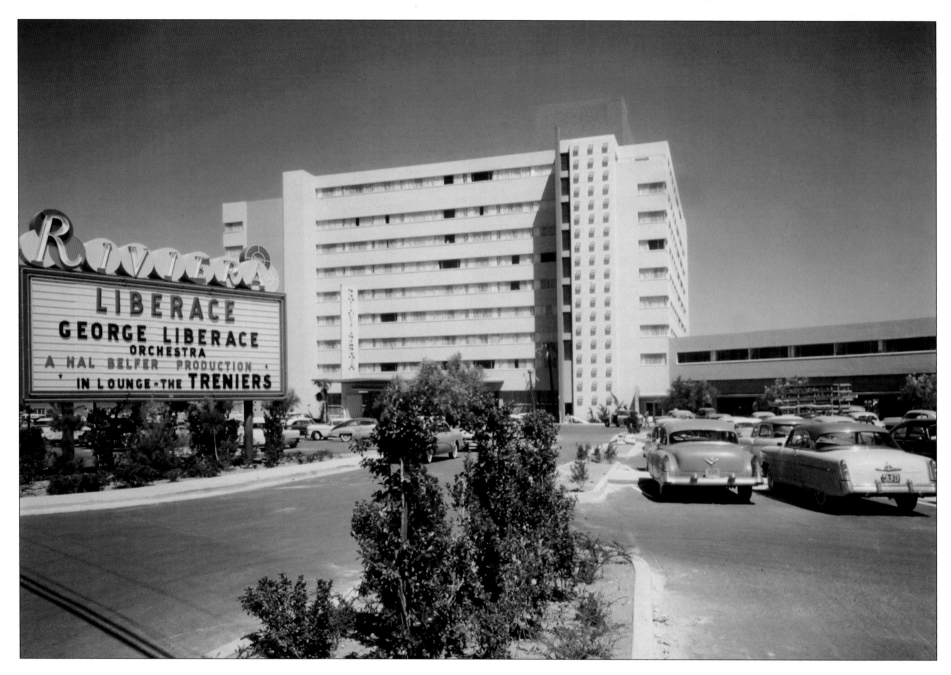

The nine-story Riviera opened on April 20, 1955, as the first high-rise on the Strip. It emphasized European splendor in its decor and was also one of the first resorts to utilize elevators. Opening act Liberace made headlines with his then unheard-of $50,000 a week salary, but its original owners went bankrupt just three months after opening, casualties of a glut of casinos opening on the Strip in 1955.

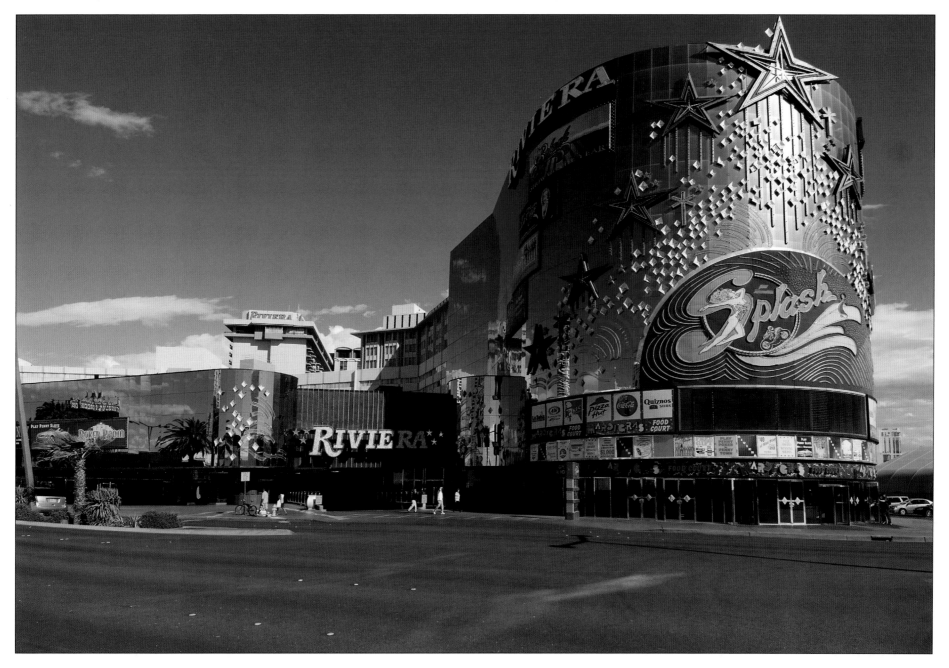

Over the years, the Riviera has managed to survive a number of financial downturns. Of the four hotels that opened in the spring of 1955, it is the only survivor. A number of renovations over the years have changed its exterior, but none as dramatically as the erection of this glass, wall-mounted neon display on the casino's facade that features colorful lighting and graphic panels. Much of the movie *Casino* was filmed here in 1995. On April 20, 2005, with fireworks off its Monaco Tower, the Riviera celebrated its fiftieth

anniversary, making it the fifth Strip property to reach the half-century mark. The Riviera's shareholders rejected a $426.5 million buyout offer in 2006, so it looks like the facility has no immediate plans to give up its heritage. A comfortable blend of new and old Las Vegas, it's a great value for Vegas visitors. Pairing the scene with fine dining and racy shows, it earns its billing as the "Entertainment Center of Las Vegas."

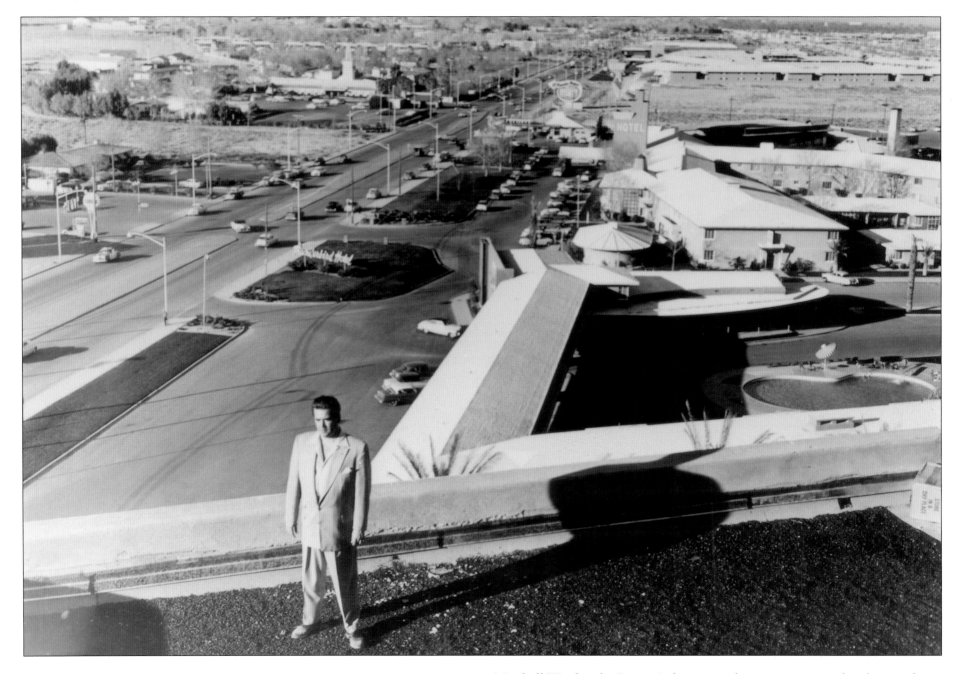

Marshall Wright, the Riviera's first general manager, surveys his domain from the rooftop of the newly constructed Riviera Hotel in 1955. Just behind Wright is the Thunderbird Hotel. North along the Strip to the left is the distinctive windmill of the El Rancho Vegas, and still further on, the Sahara Hotel is on the right.

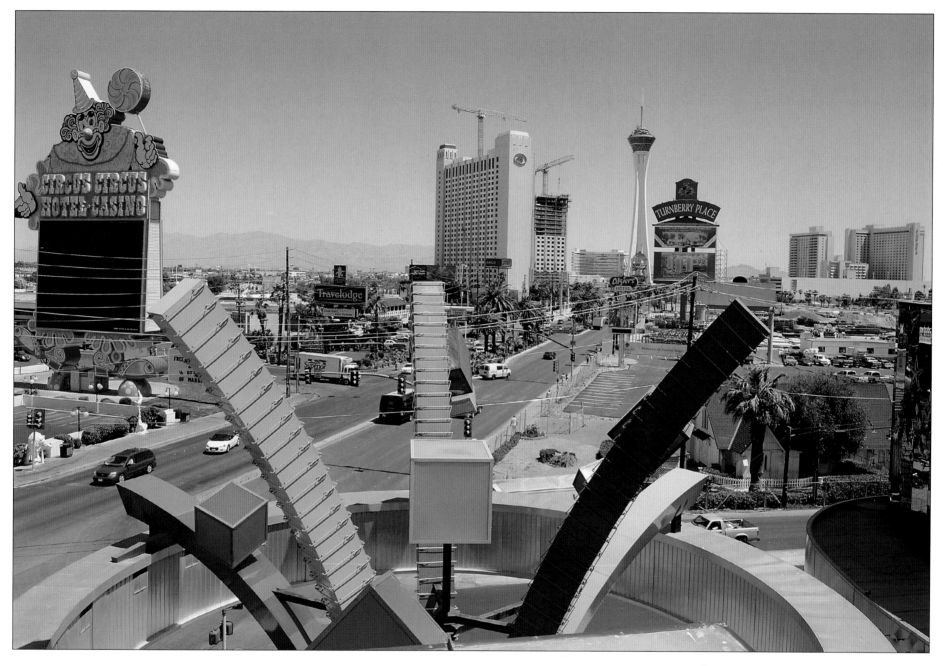

Fifty years later, the view is dramatically different, with both the El Rancho Vegas and the Thunderbird Hotel gone. Only the Sahara Hotel remains, flanked by the Turnberry Place condominiums to the south and the Wet 'n Wild water park to the north. The 1,149-foot-tall Stratosphere Tower, which calls itself "the tallest building west of the Mississippi River and tallest freestanding observation tower in the U.S.," dominates the

Strip's skyline in all directions. To the northwest, the city's development stretches as far as the eye can see. It takes a bit of imagination to envision the seemingly tough guy Marshall Wright, a one-time boxing promoter, enjoying some spaghetti and nachos at the Mexitalia restaurant in Circus Circus. But there's a little bit of old-school Wright in every Vegas casino, which is what draws 37 million visitors to Las Vegas every year.

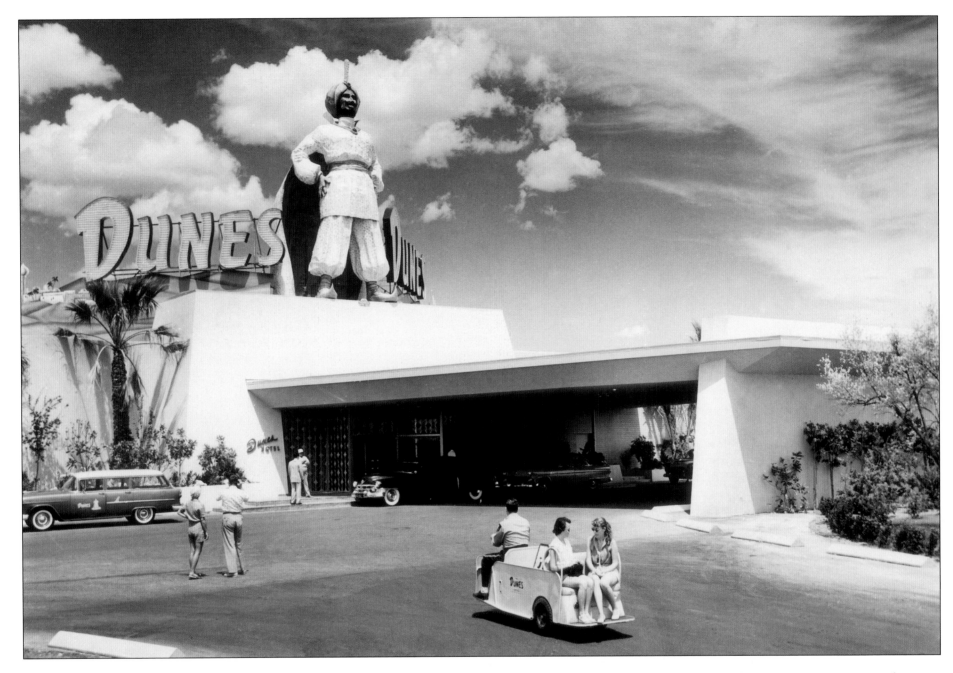

This thirty-foot-tall fiberglass sultan atop the casino entrance greeted visitors to the Dunes Hotel when it opened on May 23, 1955. Inexperienced management and competition from a number of hotels that opened in spring 1955 quickly led the Dunes into financial difficulties. The property struggled until manager Major Arteburn Riddle took over in late 1956. Riddle added a number of attractions to the hotel, including *Minsky's Follies*, the first topless revue in Las Vegas.

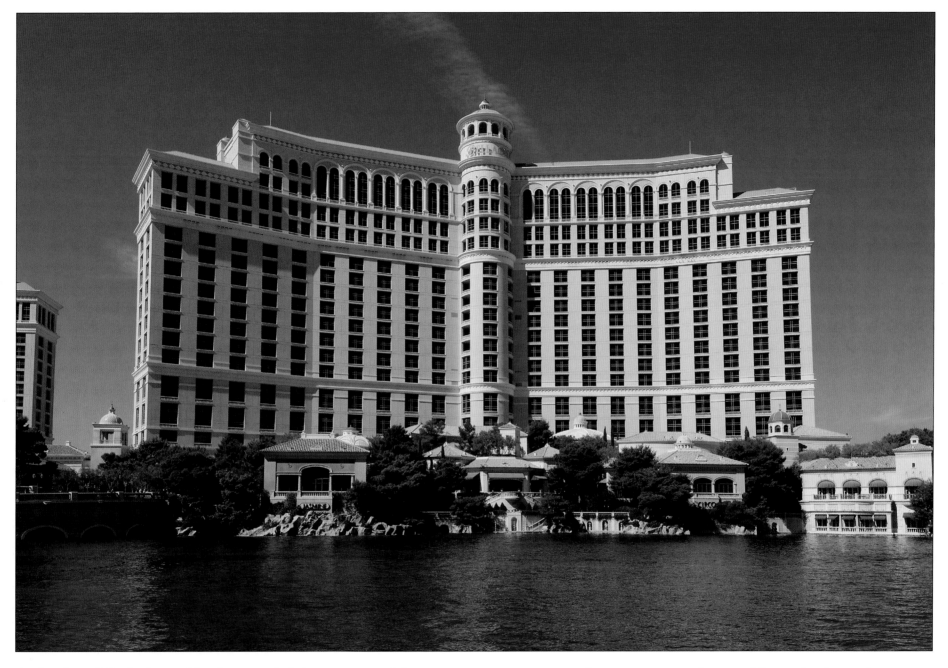

In October 1993, the Dunes Hotel was imploded in a torrent of dust and debris to make way for entrepreneur Steve Wynn's Bellagio resort. Modeled after a Tuscan village and constructed at a cost of over $1 billion, the Bellagio celebrated its grand opening on October 15, 1998. An 8.5-acre artificial lake adorns its exterior facade and a botanical garden and spectacular blown-glass ceiling by artist Dale Chihuly are among its most distinctive interior features. The market has spoken, and nearing ten years of service the Bellagio is going strong. In 2004, it unveiled over 900 additional rooms, new retail stores, more restaurants, and 60,000 extra feet of exhibition space. The Bellagio's Conservatory and Botanical Gardens, just past the lobby, are a pleasant start to your stay no matter what the weather.

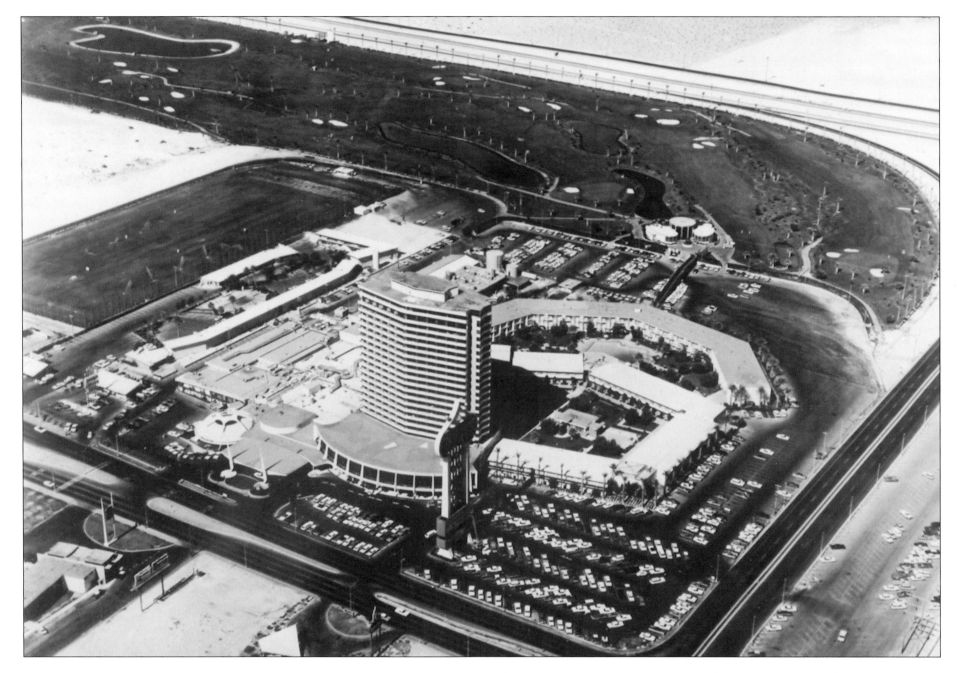

The hotel's eighteen-hole golf course looks like an oasis in the desert in this aerial view of the Dunes in the late 1960s. Located behind the golf course is Interstate 15, where the recently relocated sultan greeted drivers as they traversed the highway. Just visible at the bottom is the trademark "Diamond of the Dunes" neon sign; at 180 feet high, it was the tallest freestanding sign in the world at the time.

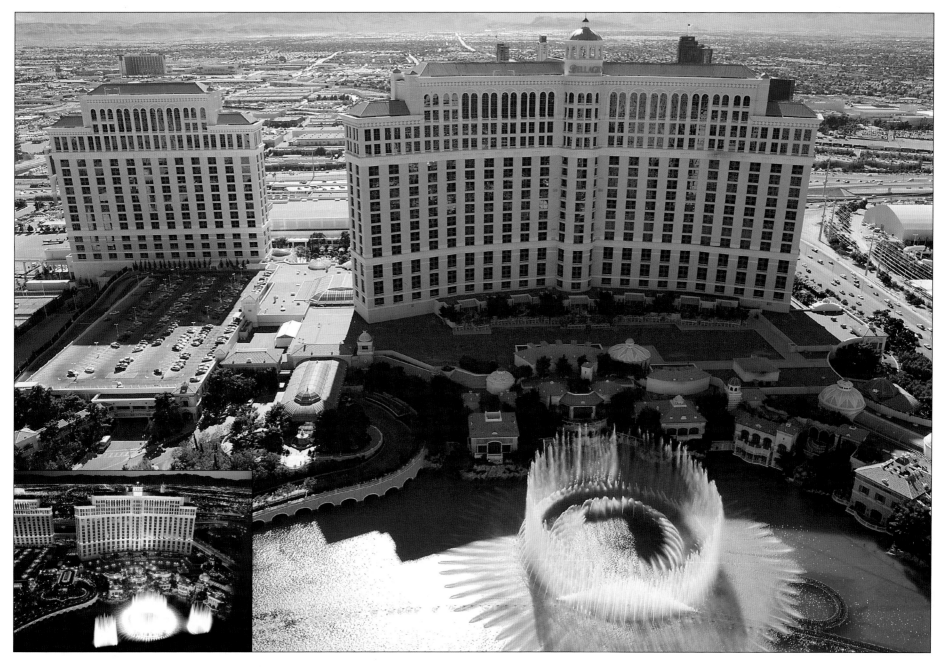

An aerial view of the lake at the Bellagio shows the outline of the fountain mechanisms that can shoot water up to 240 feet in the air. More than a thousand fountains make up the display, which entertains millions of visitors each year. Spectators gather on foot around the perimeter, even stopping Strip traffic at times. The majestic water spouts and sways to synchronized light and music, and was featured in the ending of the 2001 movie *Ocean's*

Eleven. Despite all its consumer pleasantries, or perhaps because of them, the Bellagio has become an especially popular destination for business travelers. With a generous business center, equipment rentals, mini-suite rentals, good coffee, and package deals, it makes going back to one's daily routine at the office or home a little disappointing.

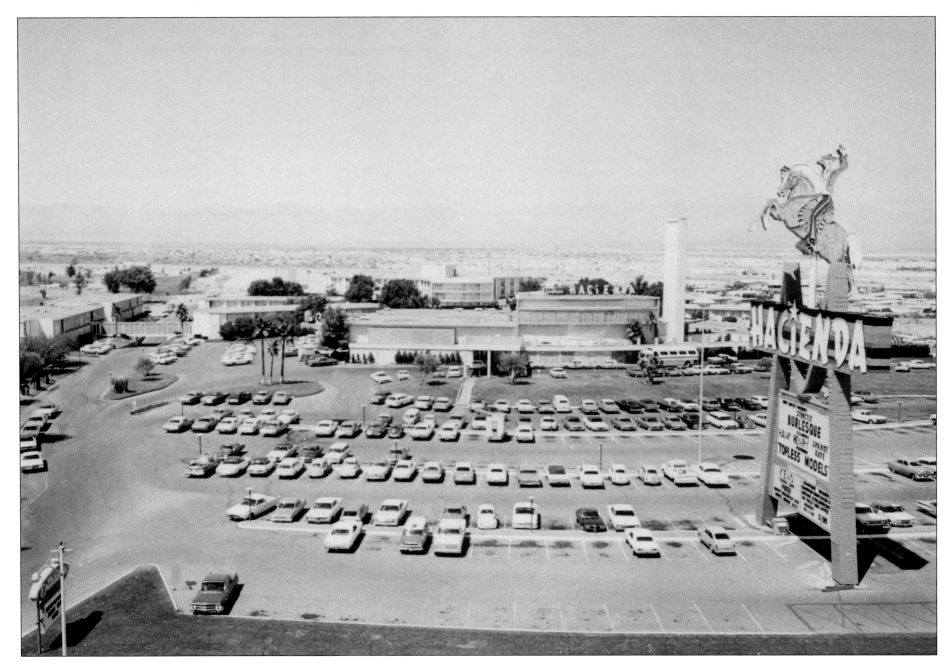

In June 1956, the Hacienda Hotel opened on the far south end of the Strip, with its trademark neon horse and rider welcoming visitors to the resort. Almost two miles from the nearest hotel, the Hacienda's isolation made survival difficult. It succeeded by sponsoring attractions such as a night-lit golf course and midget car racing. By far the most successful Hacienda promotion, however, was the creation of an air fleet to ferry passengers in from California and other U.S. cities.

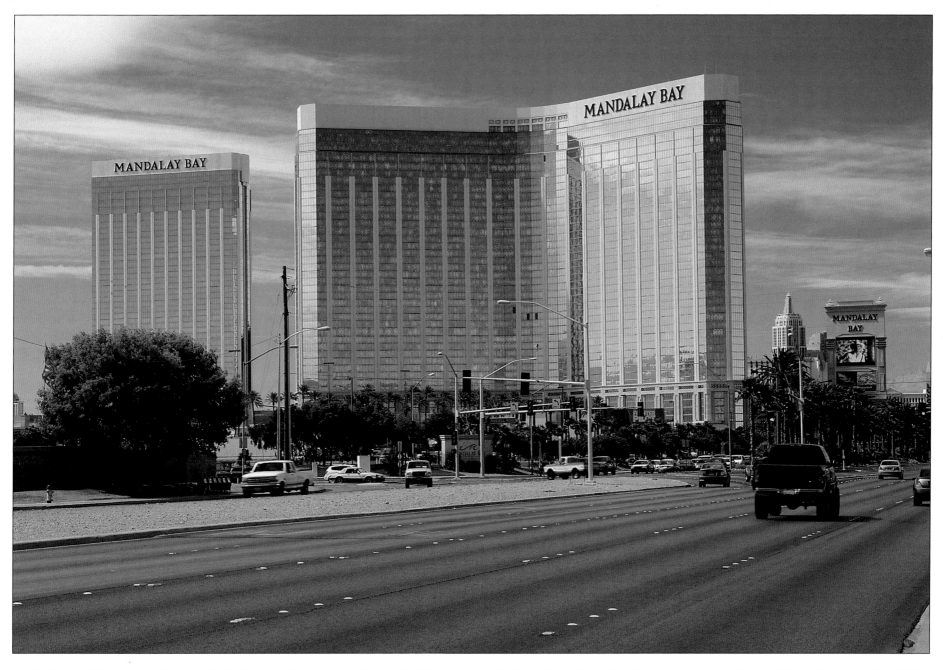

Imploded on New Year's Eve 1996, the Hacienda was one of several older hotels to be demolished in the 1990s to make way for megaresorts. It was replaced by Mandalay Bay, a luxury resort styled after an exotic South Seas island, which opened on March 3, 1999. Landscaped with over five thousand palm trees, the resort also features a sand beach with a unique wave pool that allows for adjustable waves. The second tower, forty-three stories high, is a trendy, upscale destination known as THE Hotel at

Mandalay Bay. Considered separate but under the Mandalay umbrella, THE Hotel opened the week before Christmas 2003, at the time boasting 1,100 suites that were billed as the largest standard rooms on the Strip. Mandalay Bay is owned by the MGM Mirage group, and has recently housed such popular events as the Ultimate Fighting Championship and the Professional Bull Riders World Finals.

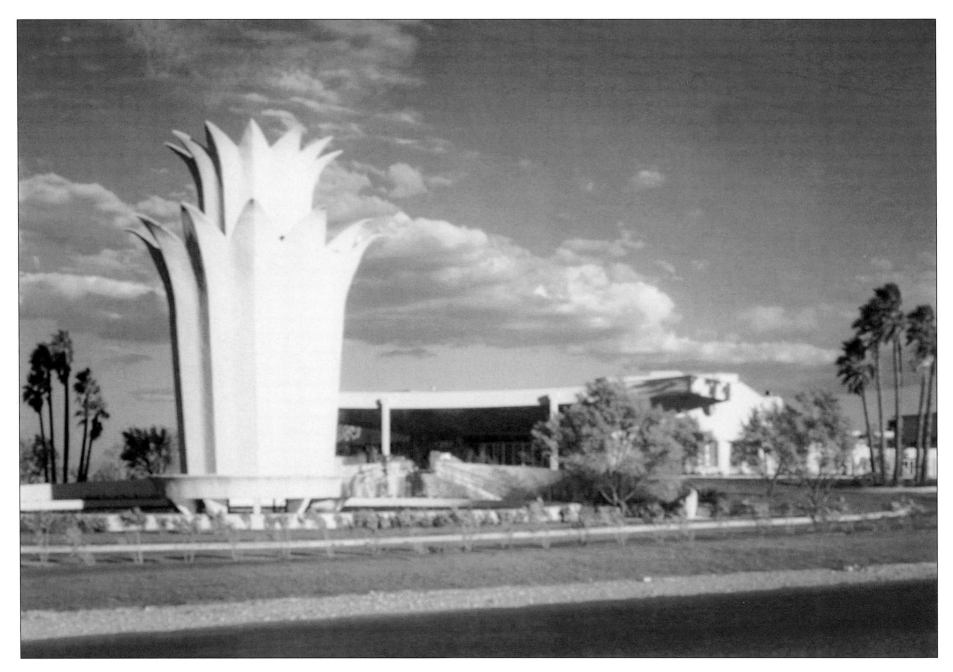

This striking sixty-foot tulip-shaped fountain was just one of the Tropicana's distinctive features when it opened on the Strip's barren south end on April 4, 1957. The Caribbean-themed resort was nicknamed the "Tiffany's of the Strip" for its elegant design and luxurious surroundings in which guests could reach their hotel rooms without going through the casino. In 1959, the Tropicana became home to the Strip's second French showgirl spectacular with the opening of the *Folies Bergere*.

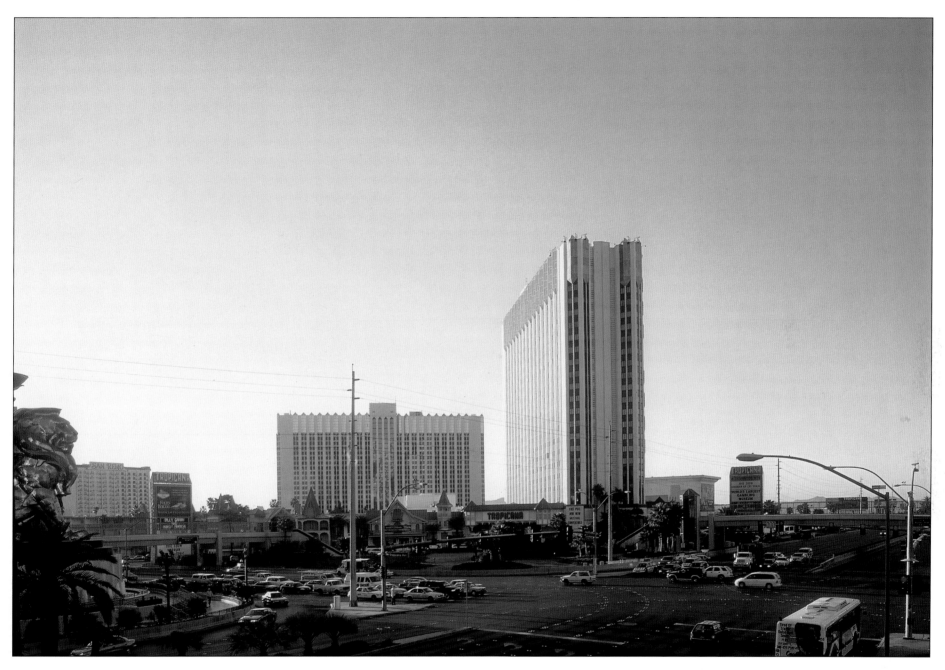

The Tropicana's trademark fountain fell victim to the wrecking ball when the hotel was remodeled in the late 1970s. The hotel's first high-rise, the twenty-two-story Tiffany Tower, was completed in 1979. In 1985, the "Island of Las Vegas" theme was unveiled, and resulted in the addition of a five-acre water oasis and another high-rise. Through it all, the Tropicana has remained home to the *Folies Bergere*—the longest-running show on the Strip. Columbia Sussex has recently acquired this prime real estate and plans a $2 billion overhaul that will leverage the brand yet update the amenities.

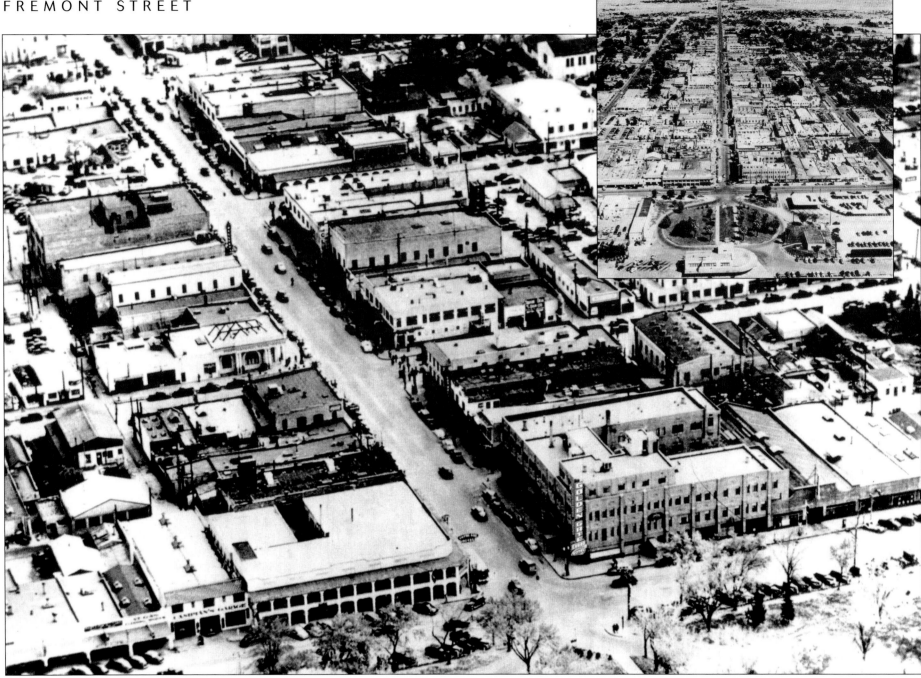

These aerial postcard views of Fremont Street, photographed in the early 1940s, show why it was the center of gambling activity in the first half of the twentieth century. The Union Pacific station is located at the bottom of the inset picture, which shows that visitors to Las Vegas would arrive at the northern end of Fremont Street. The first hotels they encountered on Fremont Street would be the Overland to the left and the Nevada to the right. The Nevada was renamed the Sal Sagev ("Las Vegas" backward) in 1931 and became the Golden Gate Hotel & Casino in 1955. The main picture, though dating from the 1940s, is a photographic anomaly. The Sal Sagev Hotel sign has been superimposed by the Golden Gate sign, which appeared in the mid-1950s.

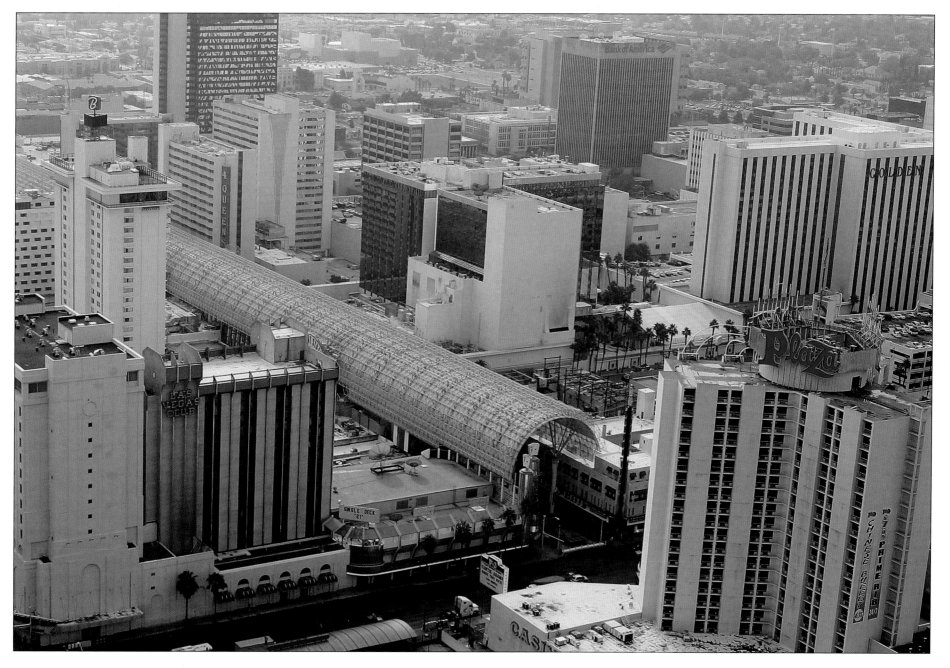

Remarkably, the Golden Gate has resisted the high-rise march of progress, although the station and gardens have not. Jackie Gaughan's Plaza Hotel was built between the station and Fremont, and opened in 1971 (see page 49), while train services through Las Vegas were suspended in 1997. The single biggest addition to the scene is the Fremont Steet roof. By the 1990s, the Strip had tilted the center of interest far south and the declining Fremont Street was in need of a makeover. In June 1992, architect Jon Jerde proposed a plan to turn the street into a pedestrian walkway and cover it all with a lighted, musical dome. Less than three years and more than $70 million later, the Fremont Street Experience opened in December 1995. Where Fremont Street was once covered in a blanket of stars that was drowned out by all the neon lights, now it is covered in a canopy 90 feet high and 1,400 feet long, which uses 12.5 million LED bulbs to put on a spectacular light and sound show every evening.

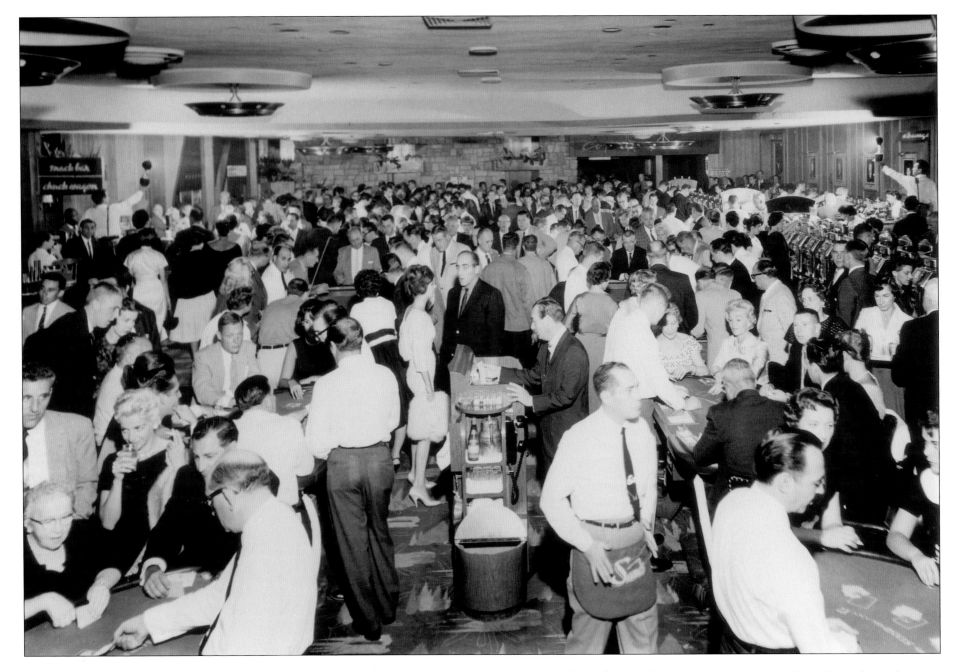

Patrons crowd the floor of the Sands casino in this photo from the early 1960s. At a time when most casinos were less than three thousand square feet in size, table games covered most of the floor, with only a few slot machines located on the side. The sea of suits, ties, furs, and pearls on the casino floor makes it clear that gambling was a dressed-up affair in early years.

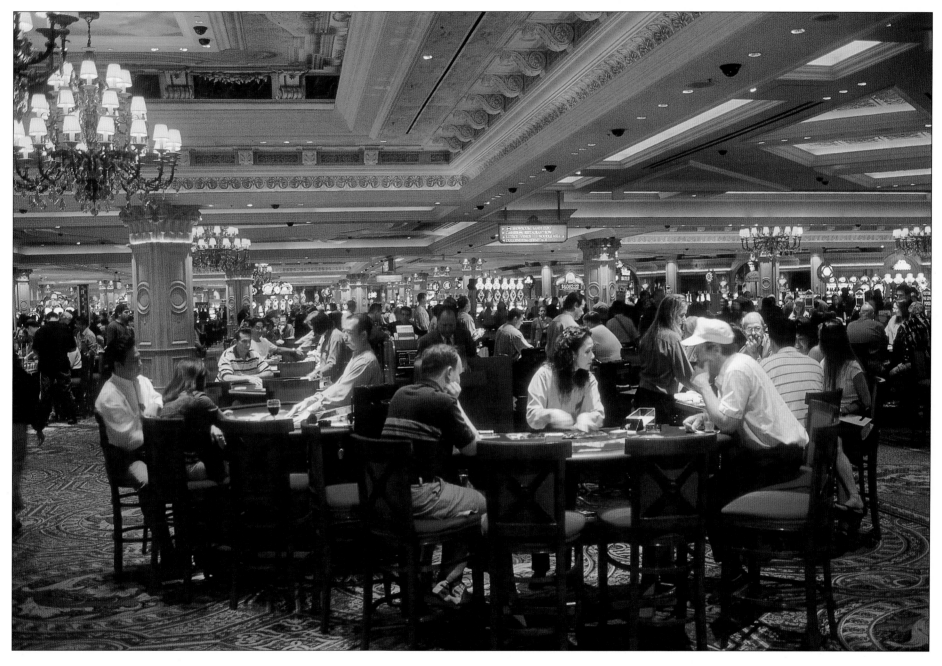

The luxurious interior of the Venetian's casino is a far cry from the densely packed casino of its predecessor, the Sands. Despite the more opulent, ornate surroundings, the casual dress of the patrons seems to indicate that gambling is no longer seen as a dress-up occasion. The facility houses a luxurious 10,000-square-foot poker room with thirty-nine tables geared for a variety of skill levels. The Venetian Poker Room's wood and leather accents give the room the feel of an Old World gentlemen's club, offering conventional games, Texas Hold 'Em, Omaha, and more. The poker room is kept smoke-free, so participants can play their best without distraction. For those who prefer to play the big time, a separate high-stakes game room is available for living large without the hoi polloi.

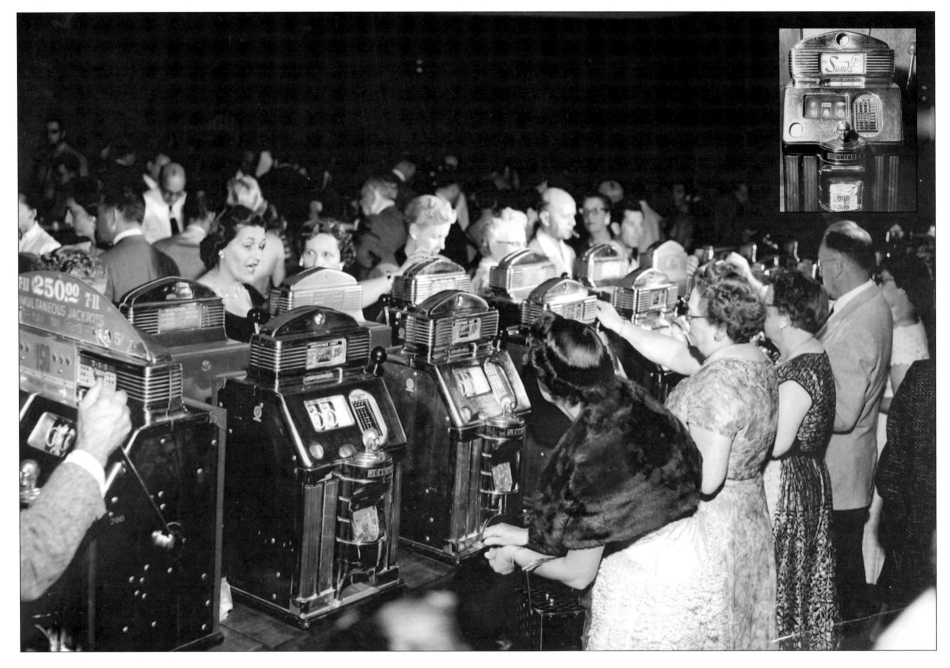

A view of the Sands casino in the early 1960s shows a small bank of slot machines played by well-dressed women. As table games were the real moneymaker for casinos in the early days of Las Vegas, slot machines were generally accorded secondary status: a distraction for the wives of men engaged in "serious gambling." A one-armed bandit (*inset*) from the Sands casino is representative of the conventional three-reeled mechanical slot machines common at the time.

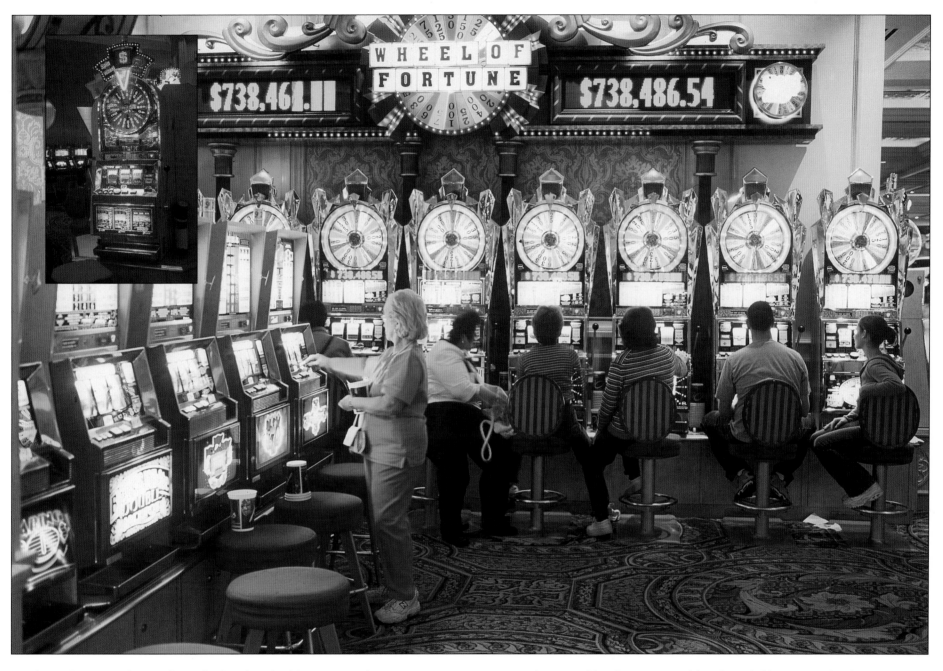

By the early 1980s, slot machines had replaced table games as the major source of revenue, accounting for as much as two-thirds of some casinos' income. With hundreds of different styles and brands of slots, these cash cows easily outnumber table games in any Las Vegas casino today. Increasingly, slot machines, such as these Wheel of Fortune machines at the Venetian (*inset*), have been themed after popular television shows and movies. In addition, the new machines, unlike the one-armed bandits of old, are completely operated by computer chips and accept paper currency. Slot machines originally managed to dodge state laws by doubling as vending machines—a stick of gum was "purchased" with every coin. That's why the machines employ fruit symbols rather than playing card symbols. Lemons were said to be bad luck; hence, an unreliable car or other product came to be known as a "lemon."

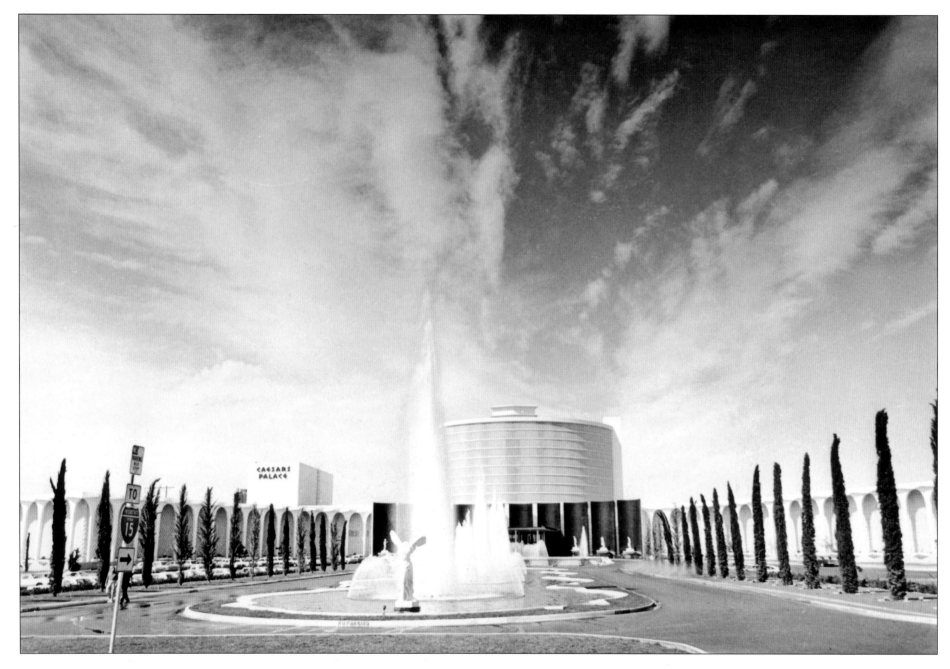

A monument to Las Vegas excess, Caesars Palace celebrated its grand opening on August 5, 1966, with a party that topped $1 million. Its distinctive Greco-Roman design included some eighteen huge fountains, a 135-foot drive lined with imported Italian cypresses, and more than $150,000 worth of imported marble statuary from Italy. Complementing the hotel's fourteen-story high-rise was the 980-seat Circus Maximus Showroom, which had been patterned after the Colosseum in Rome. Jay Sarno, the larger-than-life creator of Caesars Palace, was also the driving force behind another early themed resort, the family-oriented Circus Circus, which opened across from the Riviera in 1968.

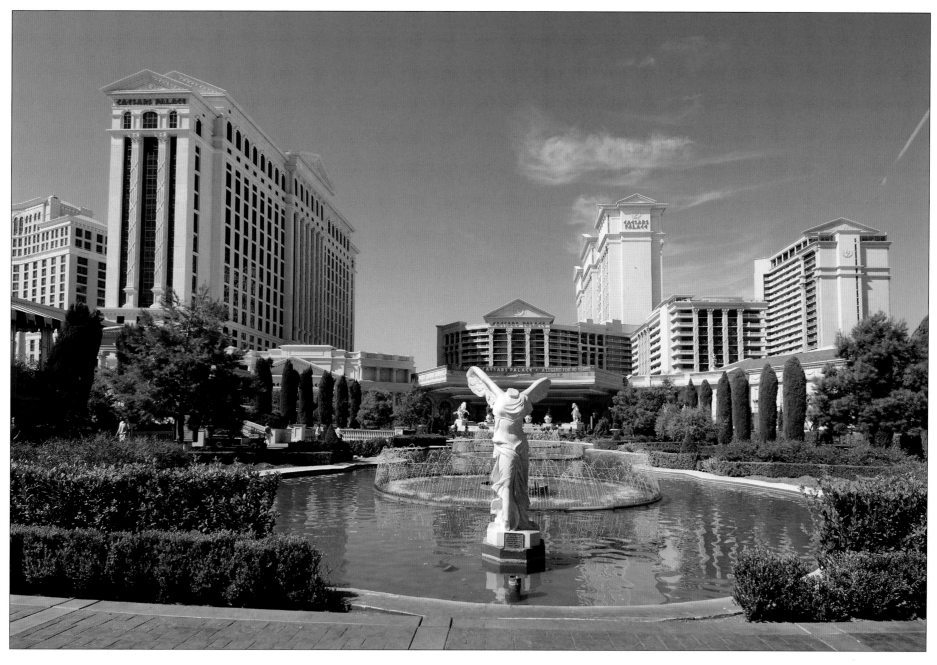

Although the replica of the Winged Victory of Samothrace continues to greet visitors to Caesars Palace over forty years later, much of the hotel's exterior has changed dramatically. Between 1970 and 1979, three high-rises joined the original tower, and the twenty-six-story Palace Tower was added in 1997. Another addition to the original resort, the lavish Forum Shops at Caesars, has been a favorite haunt of celebrities visiting Las Vegas since its opening in May 1992. Today, Caesars is yet another big brand that falls under the Harrah's banner. And they don't get much bigger. In addition to high-rolling games and some of the swankest suites of the Strip, acts like Elton John, Jerry Seinfeld, and Celine Dion hit Caesars' stages every week. The Arts & Entertainment Television Network produced a reality TV series about the casino in 2004.

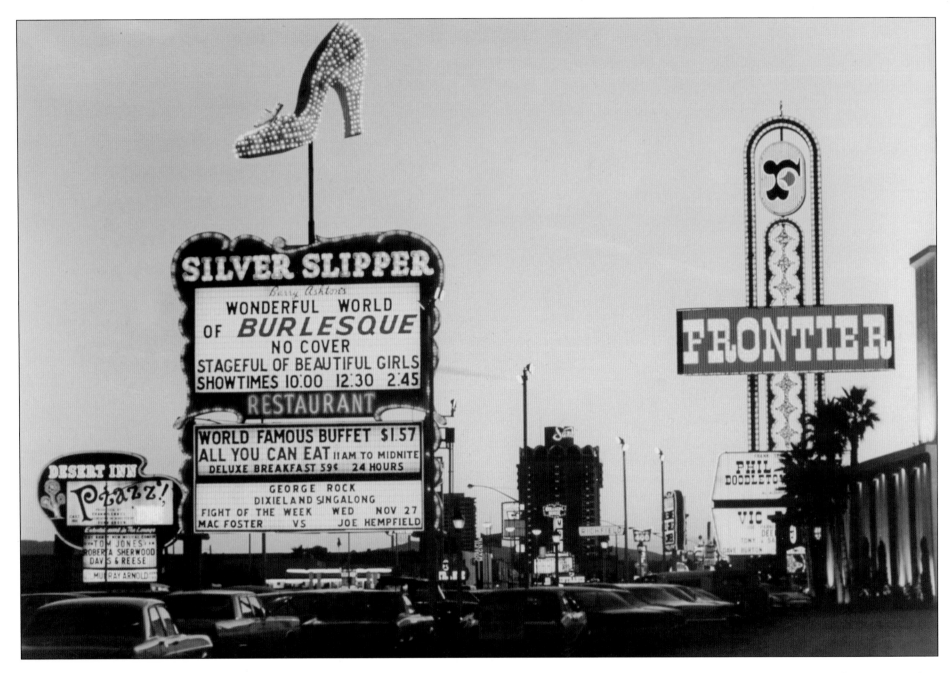

Built as part of the Last Frontier Village in 1942, the Silver Slipper opened as a separate casino in 1950. One of five Strip casinos purchased by Howard Hughes between 1966 and 1970, the Silver Slipper's acquisition was the stuff of Hughes's legend. Living opposite the hotel on the Desert Inn's tenth floor, Hughes reportedly became exasperated by the red glow cast by the rotating neon shoe and decided to buy it just so he could tear it down.

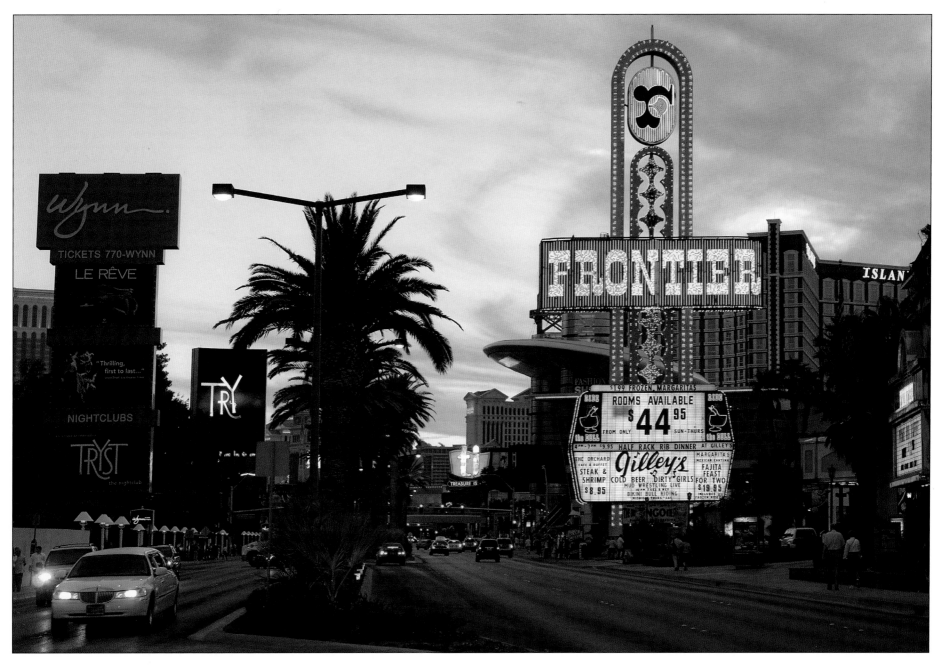

Hughes's Summa Corporation sold the Silver Slipper in June 1988 and the casino closed its doors later that year. After the building was demolished, the site where the Silver Slipper once stood was converted into additional parking for the Frontier Hotel. The distinctive neon shoe was removed and taken to the Boneyard, the resting place for Las Vegas's defunct neon, but it now glows again as part of the Las Vegas Neon Museum. While one piece of Vegas culture on the block was lost, the Wynn Collection is making up the balance. One of the top private art collections in the world, it features works by Picasso, van Gogh, Renoir, Monet, Matisse, Gauguin, Rembrandt, and Sargent.

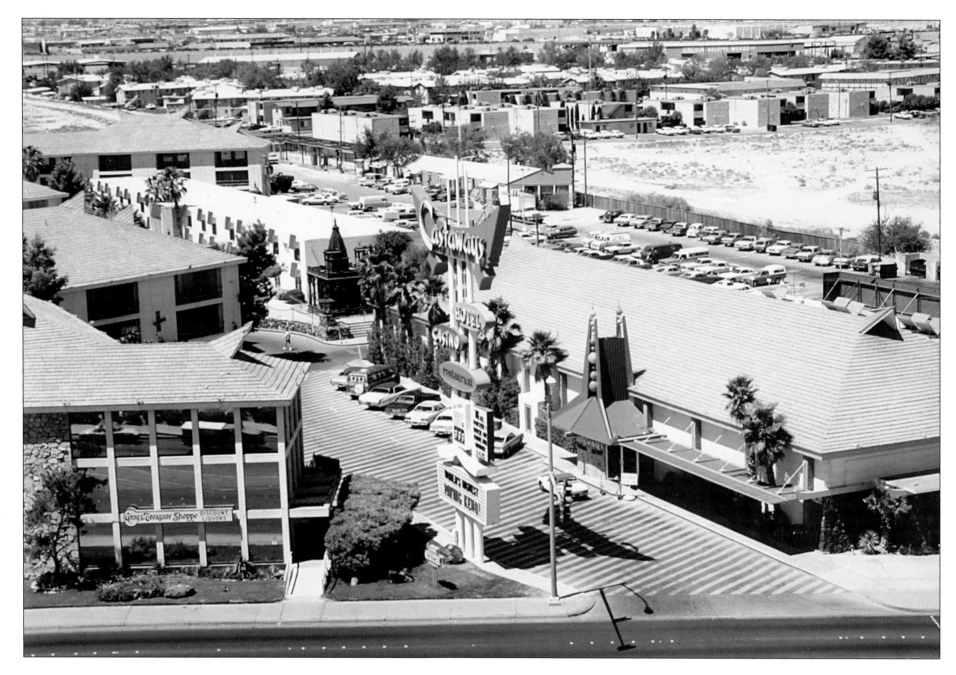

This small Polynesian-themed casino-hotel, located directly across the street from the Sands, billed itself as a "private island in the center of the Strip." It had originally opened as the Sans Souci in October 1957, but changed its name to the Castaways in 1964 and became known for its two-story honeymoon suites. The fourteen-ton teakwood "Gateway to Luck" replica of an Indian temple that was located on the hotel grounds can be seen toward the back.

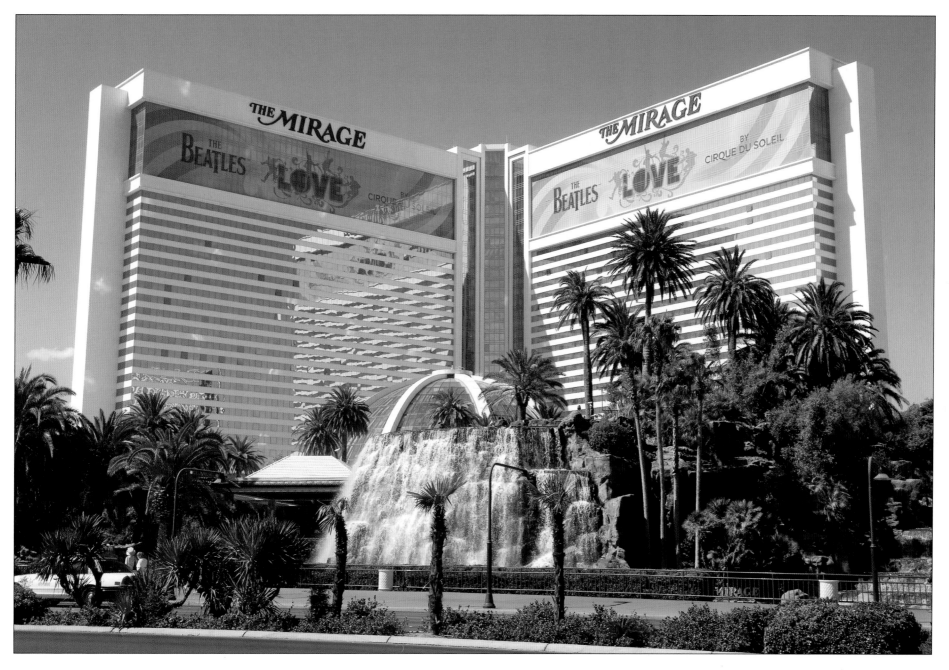

The Castaways closed in July 1987 to make way for the construction of Steve Wynn's Mirage. The luxury hotel with its shimmering, Y-shaped golden tower opened in November 1989, and is credited with starting the building renaissance that reinvigorated Las Vegas in the 1990s. Neon is noticeably absent from the Mirage's design, replaced by more tangible attractions such as the flaming volcano and Siegfried and Roy's Secret Garden and Dolphin Habitat. With or without Siegfried and Roy's long-running act, the Mirage is magical. In 2000, another casino—previously the Showboat—bought the Castaways name and theme for an undisclosed amount. Formerly the Showboat, the new Castaways lasted just a few years before declaring bankruptcy with $50 million in debt. The new Castaways was imploded in 2006.

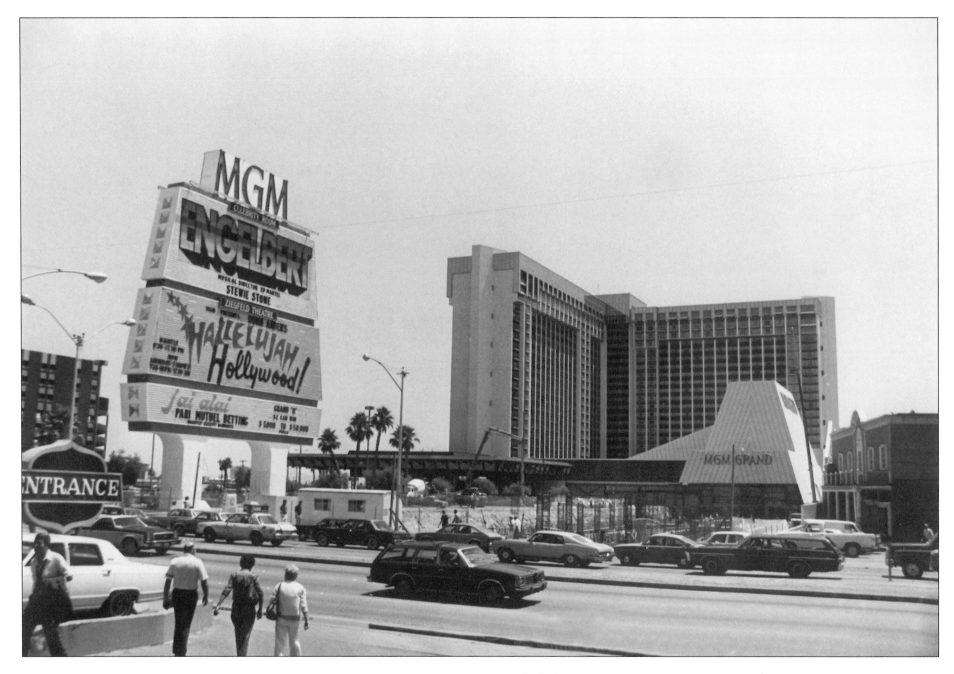

Built by billionaire Kirk Kerkorian at a cost of $106 million, the twenty-six-story MGM Grand opened on December 5, 1973. With 2,100 rooms and an interior decor patterned on the film *Grand Hotel*, the MGM Grand brought large-scale class and elegance to the Strip. On November 21, 1980, a fire broke out at the hotel, killing eighty-five people—the second-largest loss of life in a hotel fire in U.S. history.

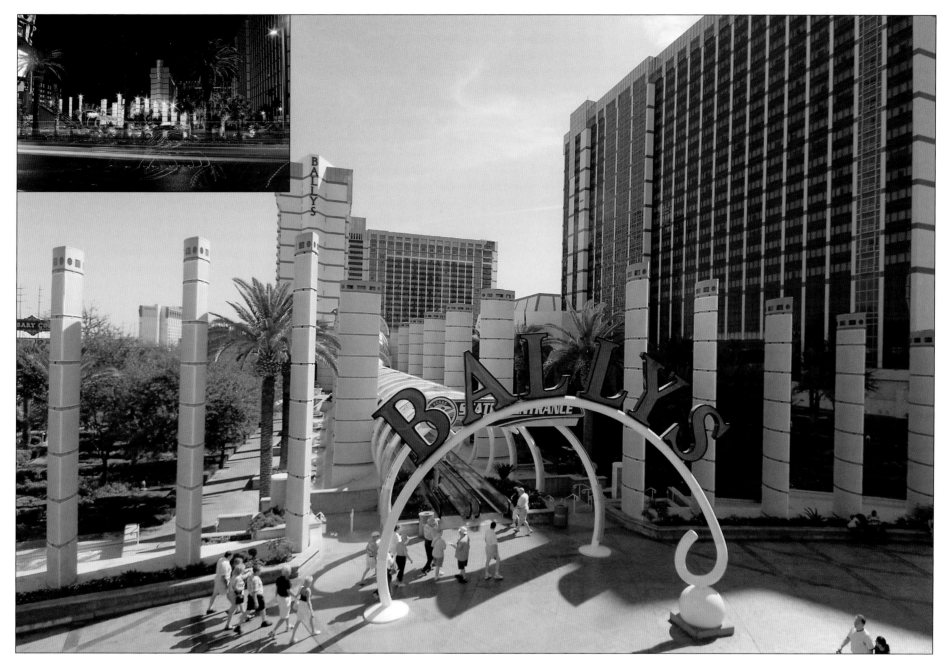

As a result of the MGM Grand tragedy, fire safety laws and building codes were changed around the country. The hotel was totally rebuilt, and in 1986 it was sold to the Bally Entertainment Corporation, which in 1994 constructed the twirling neon spiral walkway seen here. Lacking a major theme to compete with the newer megaresorts, Bally's cultivates an aura of old-time Vegas style and glamour withits slogan, "Real. Live. Las Vegas." The MGM Grand Hotel & Casino lives on at 3799 Las Vegas Boulevard; it is an MGM-Mirage-owned facility that is one of the most popular casinos in town.

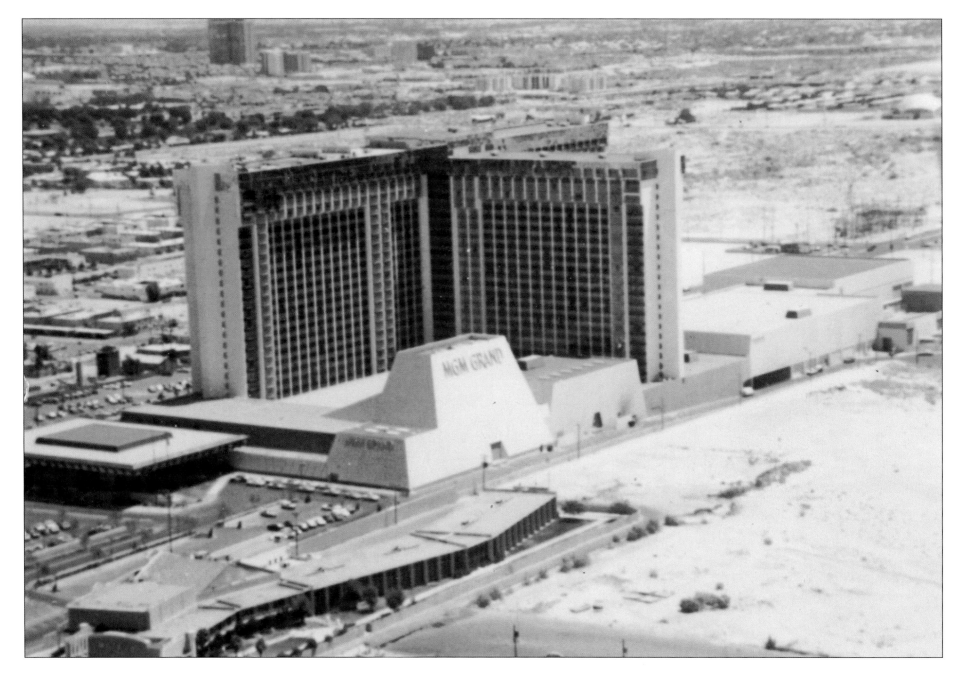

In 1975, the MGM Grand dwarfed its neighbors. The Flamingo still lacked a high-rise and the lot adjacent to the twenty-six-story hotel was populated by a small motel and a strip mall. Despite the towering elegance of the MGM Grand, the desert character of the town is still apparent in the surrounding landscape.

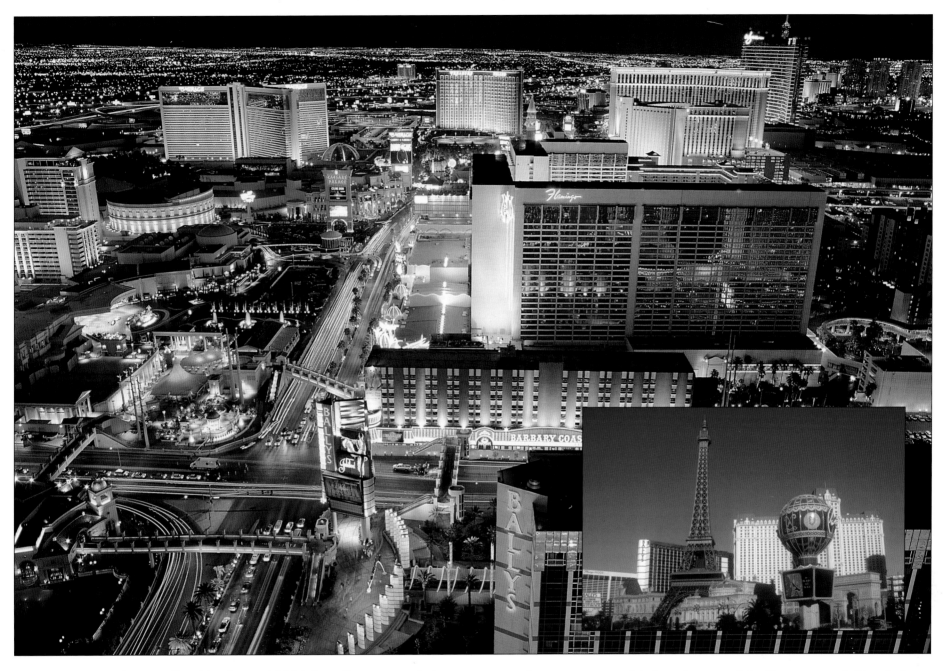

Some thirty years later, Bally's (the former MGM Grand) announced plans to construct a Paris-themed resort on the property located just south of their hotel. The hotel opened on September 1, 1999, with an exterior that featured replicas of the Eiffel Tower, Arc de Triomphe, and Paris Opera House (*inset*). The two casinos not only share a common parking garage but are connected indoors by way of the European-style Rue de la Paix shopping promenade. For those not up for the City of Light within the City of Neon, you can still hit the new MGM Grand for some of the most popular musical billings in town, including the Rolling Stones, Jimmy Buffett, Aerosmith, and more.

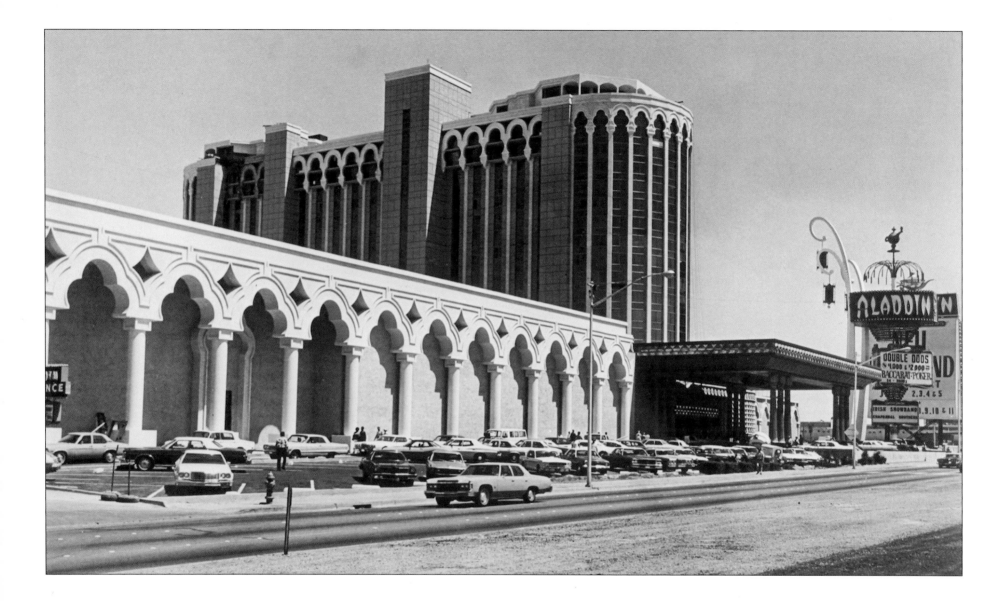

This is the second version of the Aladdin as it looked shortly after its completion in June 1976. The original, built by former Sahara owner Milton Prell, opened on April 1, 1966, on the site of the failed Tally Ho Resort. The Arabian-themed resort became famous as the site of Elvis Presley's wedding in May 1967, and gained notoriety when alleged ties to Midwest mobsters led Nevada gaming officials to briefly close the casino on August 6, 1979.

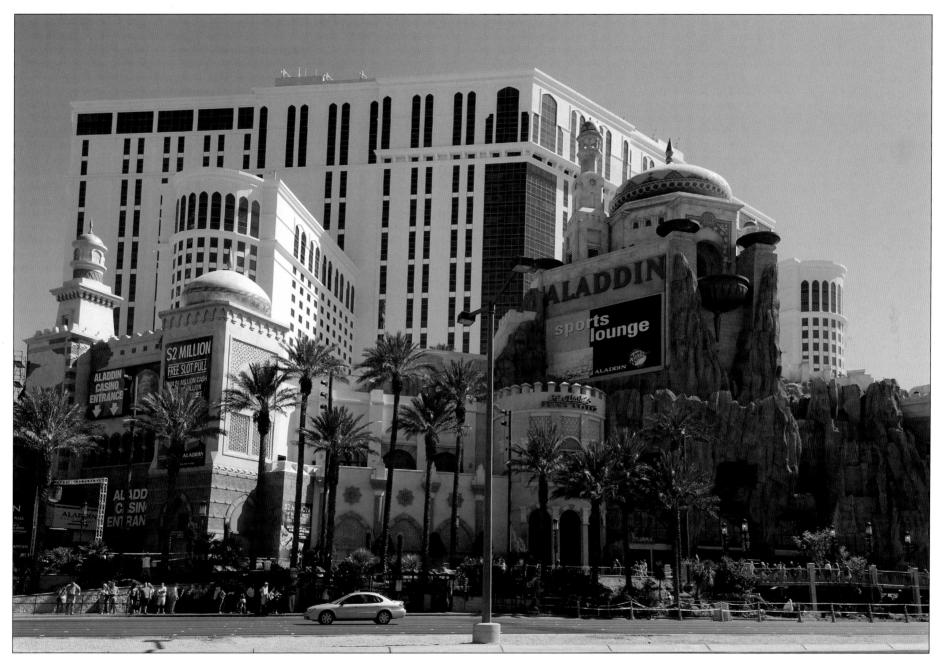

On April 27, 1998, the Aladdin was removed to make way for a luxurious new Aladdin Hotel and Casino with expanded retail and entertainment facilities. The new version opened in August 2000, its outer facade framed by palm trees and styled after a Moorish castle. Past the sumptuous Spice Market Buffet beckons the enormous, half-million-square-foot Desert Passage shopping center. Along with more than a hundred retail destinations—proclaimed to have "the most shopping options of any Las Vegas Strip resort"—is a harbor complete with a freighter and artificial fog and thunder. The property covers thirty-five acres and was built at a cost of $1.2 billion. The Aladdin's wedding chapel still draws a crowd based on its kitschy distinction as the site where Elvis and Priscilla Presley were married in 1967. More recently, the hotel has drawn crowds through top performers, the Miss America pageant, and a boxing camp run by Mike Tyson.

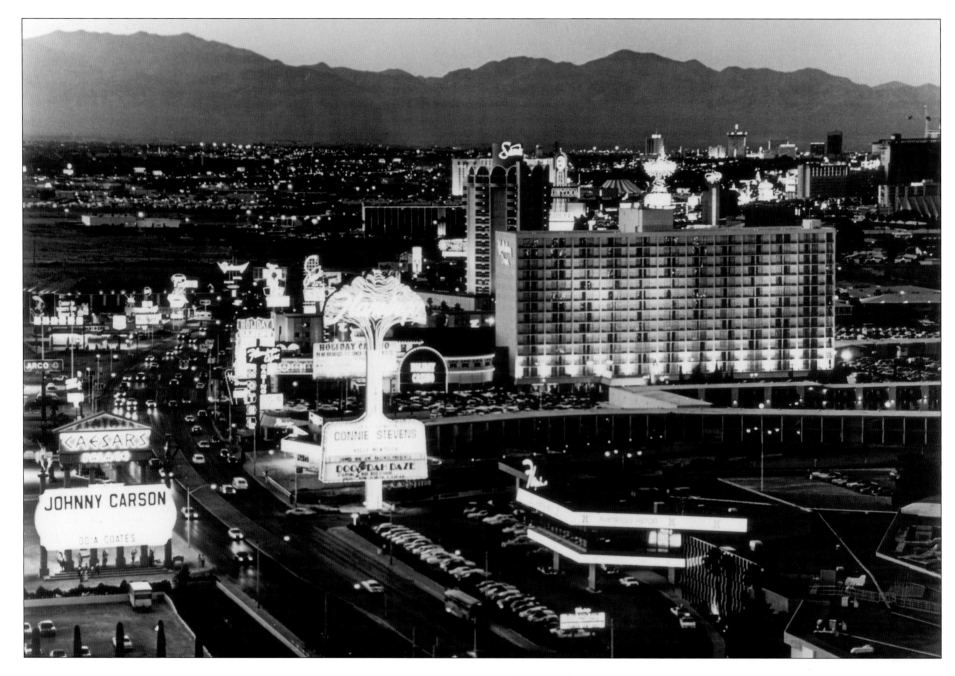

A glittering view of Las Vegas Boulevard at night, looking north from its intersection with Flamingo in the early 1970s. High-rises have begun to sprout up along the Strip, sprinkled in among the small motels and gas stations that still flank the street. Among the neon signs that glow prominently along the Strip is the Caesars Palace marquee with its trademark Greco-Roman design.

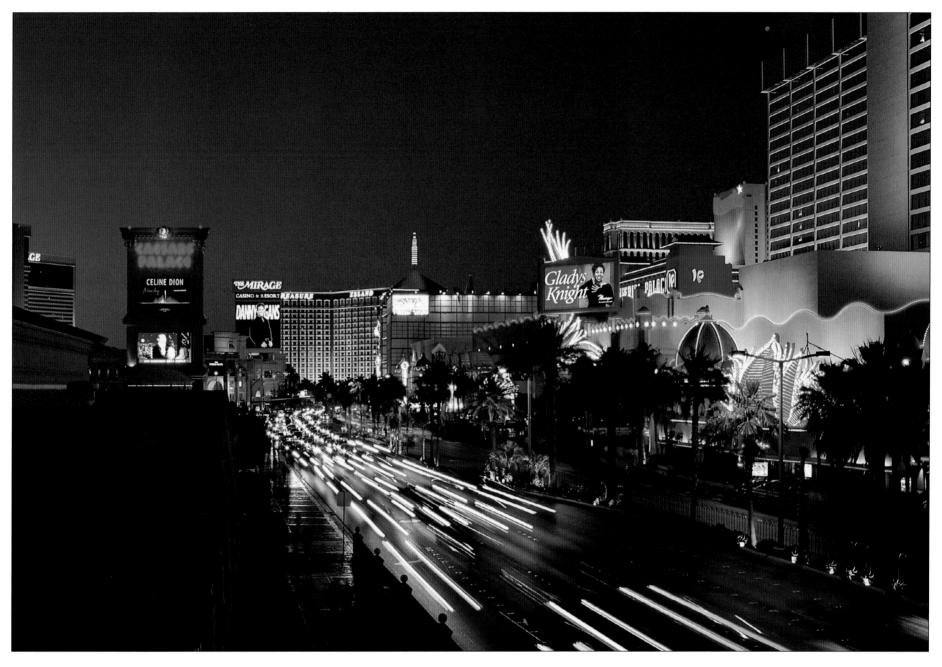

Some thirty years later, the Caesars Palace marquee still figures prominently in the Strip's landscape, but a series of high-rises and signs has altered the skyline. The Mirage and its neighbor, the thirty-six-story, pirate-themed Treasure Island resort, loom in the distance. Across the way on the east side of the Strip, the Imperial Palace Hotel, with its Chinese temple facade, obscures the neighboring Venetian from view. In 2005, $370 million bought gaming megalith Harrah's the Imperial Palace, bumping up the company's prime Vegas estate to nearly 300 acres. Major changes are afoot for the Imperial Palace, as some analysts referred to the purchase as a "vacant land sale" based on estimations of the Imperial Palace's financial performance. But you'd never know that it's a property in transition by the steady crowds enjoying themselves each evening.

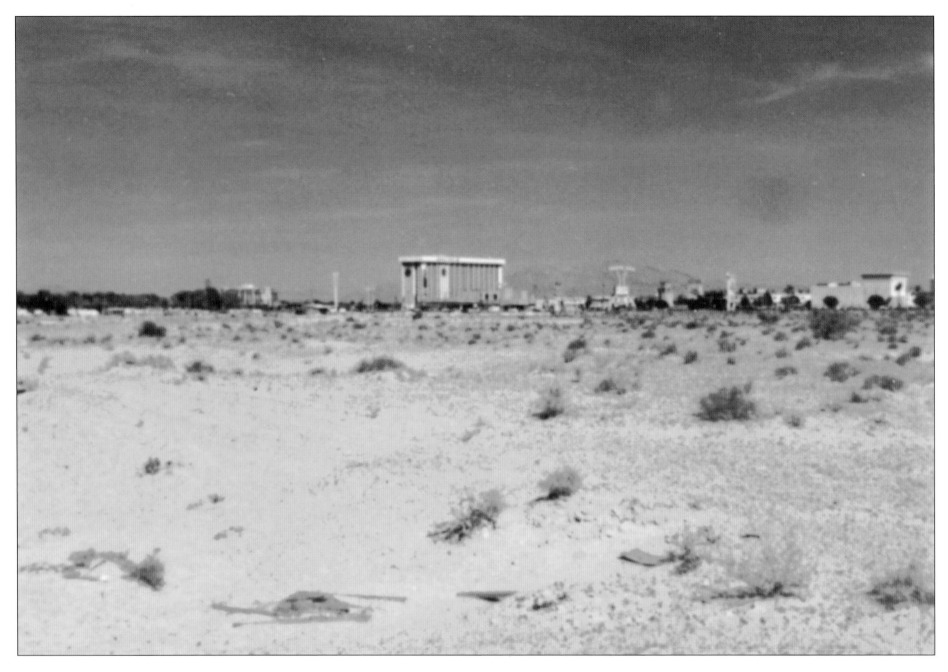

In 1975, real estate developers looking to construct the Xanadu Resort on the south end of the Strip took this photograph from the west corner of an empty lot bounded by Tropicana to the north and Las Vegas Boulevard to the east. The high-rise tower in the distance is the Marina Hotel; the Tropicana Hotel fountain is barely visible across from it.

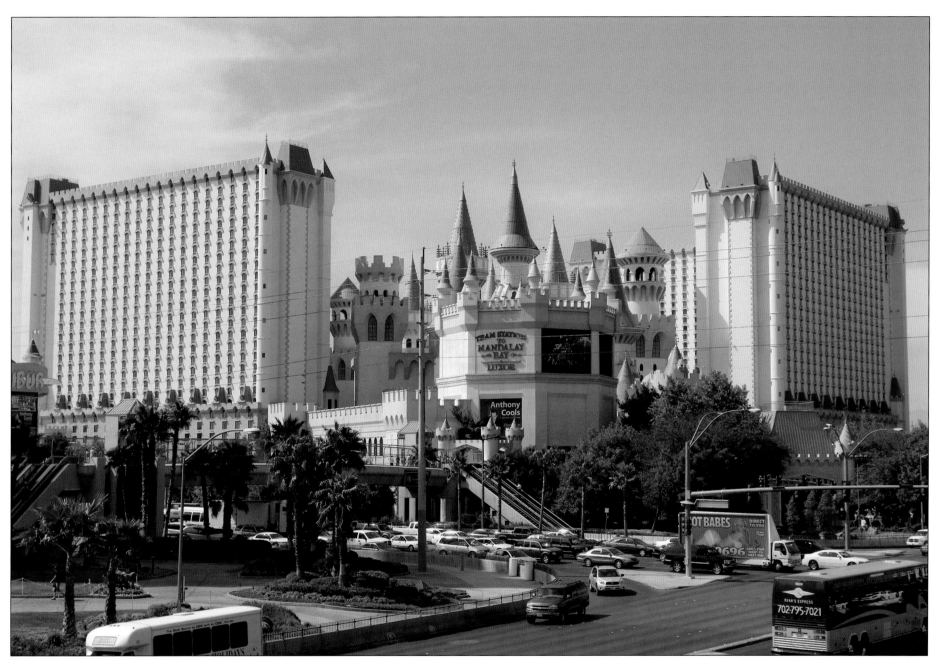

Although plans to develop the Xanadu Resort ultimately failed, this corner eventually became home to the Excalibur Hotel and Casino in June 1990. One of the Strip's most family-friendly resorts, the Excalibur was designed to resemble a medieval castle and its interior decor is patterned after the legend of King Arthur and the Knights of the Round Table. The Excalibur's distinctive castle turrets, sandwiched between massive towers housing over 4,000 rooms, are prominent in this view taken from the back of the hotel. One would think a fairy-tale theme wouldn't be enough to compete these days, but it certainly is. The casino has mastered the blend of family-friendly fun, such as the Tournament of Kings dinner show, and quality adult entertainment like comedian Louie Anderson and the Australian male revue *Thunder from Down Under*.

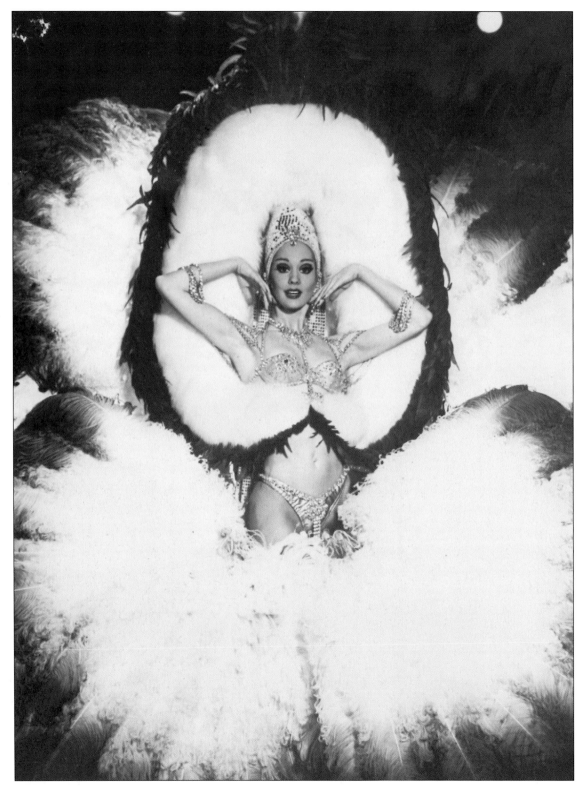

The epitome of glamour and sex appeal, the showgirl has long been a fixture in Las Vegas entertainment. Early Strip hotels such as the El Rancho Vegas and Desert Inn had chorus lines, but it was the arrival of the Stardust's spectacular French import *Lido* in 1958 that gave icon status to the statuesque beauties. In this 1978 photo from the opening number of the Stardust's *Allez Lido*, the principal dancer poses amid a sea of feathers, fur, and sequins.

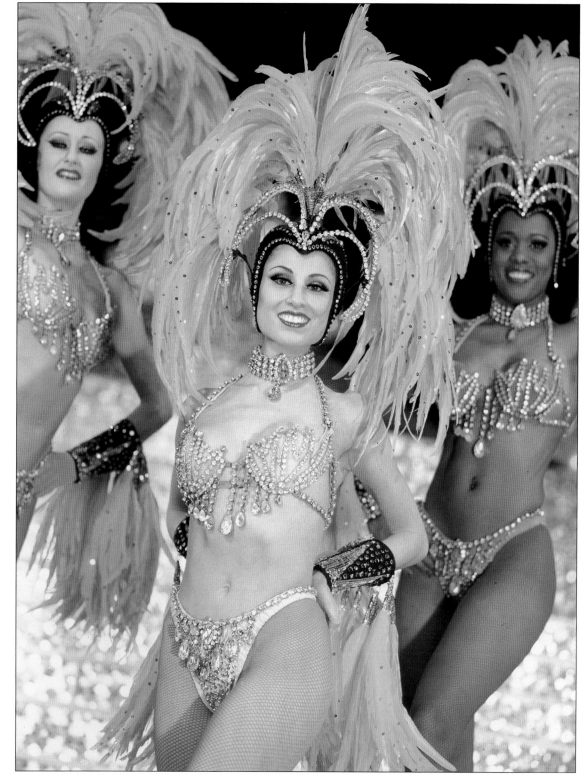

Three showgirls from the long-running *Jubilee* production show at Bally's Hotel and Casino defy the notion that the showgirl is an endangered species in modern Las Vegas. Attempts to turn the city into a family-friendly resort center in the 1990s resulted in the loss of some traditional Vegas-style entertainment, but the flash of sequins and feathers in shows such as the *Folies Bergere* and *Jubilee* continue to attract the crowds. No matter the level of spectacle, Las Vegas will always maintain a core following of the old-school sensual charm of the Strip. The Jubilee Theater draws huge crowds of men and women alike to see the showgirls and showboys—yes, that's the term—perform what's become a Las Vegas tradition.

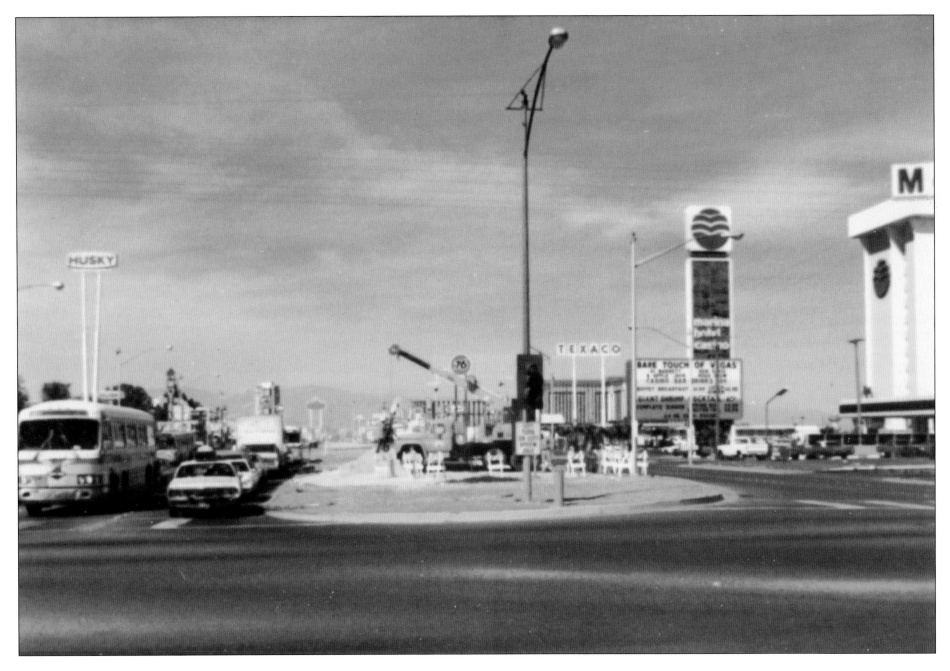

This 1975 view looks north on Las Vegas Boulevard from its intersection with Tropicana. The Marina Hotel is barely visible on the northeast corner. Gas stations and small motels flank the sides of the Strip with only a few hotel high-rises visible in the distance.

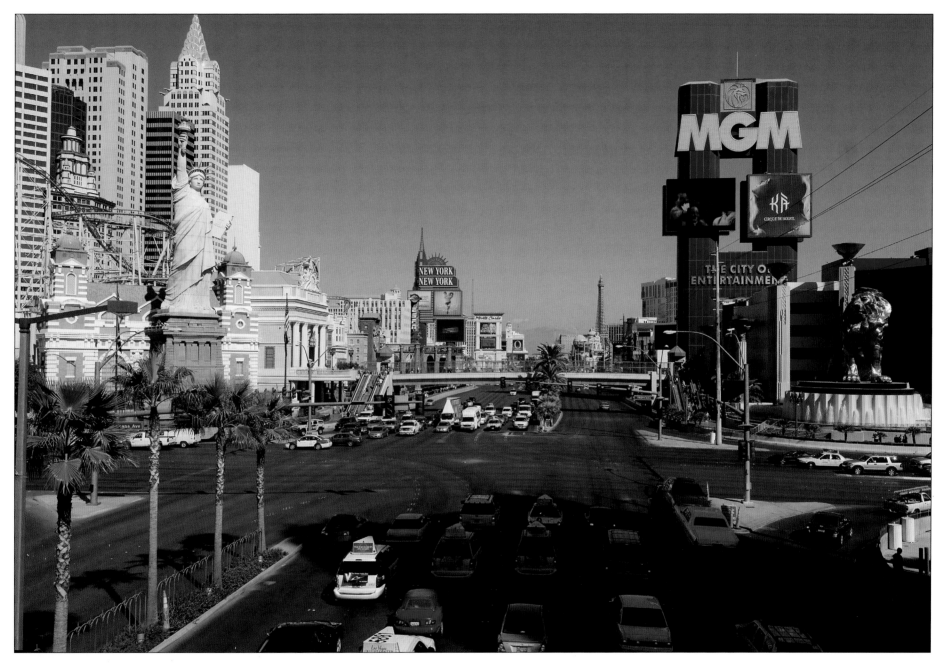

A dramatic vista of the modern-day Strip looking north, its surreal skyline is filled with towering signs and high-rises. The New York New York Hotel's Statue of Liberty replica anchors the northwest corner, and visible in the distance is the Paris Hotel's Eiffel Tower replica. The pedestrian bridge spanning across the two hotels was an innovation developed in the late 1990s, designed to reduce traffic congestion on the Strip while providing safe passage for pedestrians. With more foot traffic along the Strip each year, moving people—and their money—up, down, and to Las Vegas Boulevard efficiently is becoming more of a priority. On the east side of the Strip, a monorail was built from Tropicana Avenue to Sahara Road. Buses, trolleys, limousines, and cable-pulled trams can all be seen on the Strip.

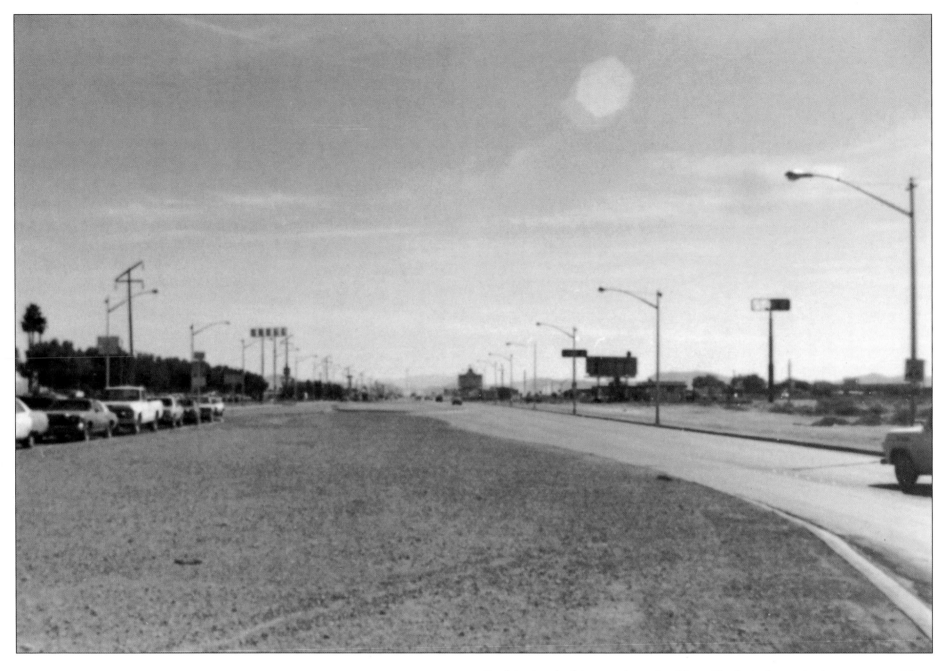

In this view looking south on Las Vegas Boulevard near its intersection with Tropicana Avenue, the Hacienda Hotel stands alone in the distance. Virtually undeveloped at this time, the southern portion of the Strip is sprinkled with only a handful of motels and gas stations in this 1975 photograph.

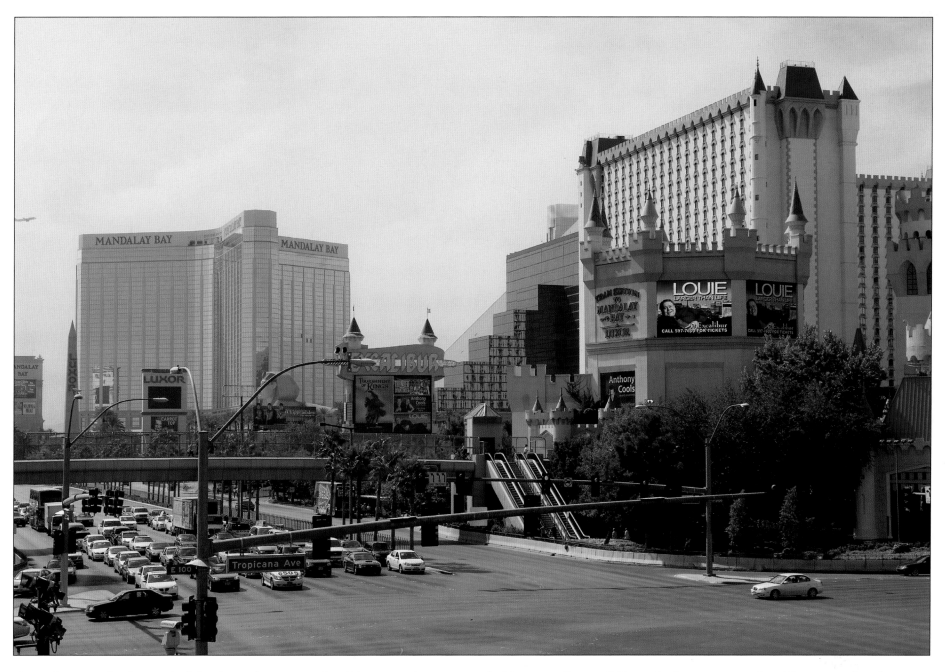

Once the more desolate end of the Strip, the area south of Tropicana Avenue is now home to three of the Strip's most colorful and lively hotels. Built in rapid succession, the castle-themed Excalibur and the Egyptian-themed Luxor, with its black glass pyramid-shaped hotel tower, were completed in 1990 and 1993, respectively. The Luxor contains 4,400 rooms (second on the Strip only to the MGM Grand) and a vast indoor atrium space theoretically capable of holding nine Boeing 747s stacked atop one another. The pyramid is also topped by the most powerful beam of light in the world, a forty-billion-candlepower xenon beam potentially visible to planes at cruising altitude 250 miles away in Los Angeles. The Luxor's elevators move at an angle rather than straight up and down. The tropically themed Mandalay Bay opened on the former site of the Hacienda Hotel in 1999.

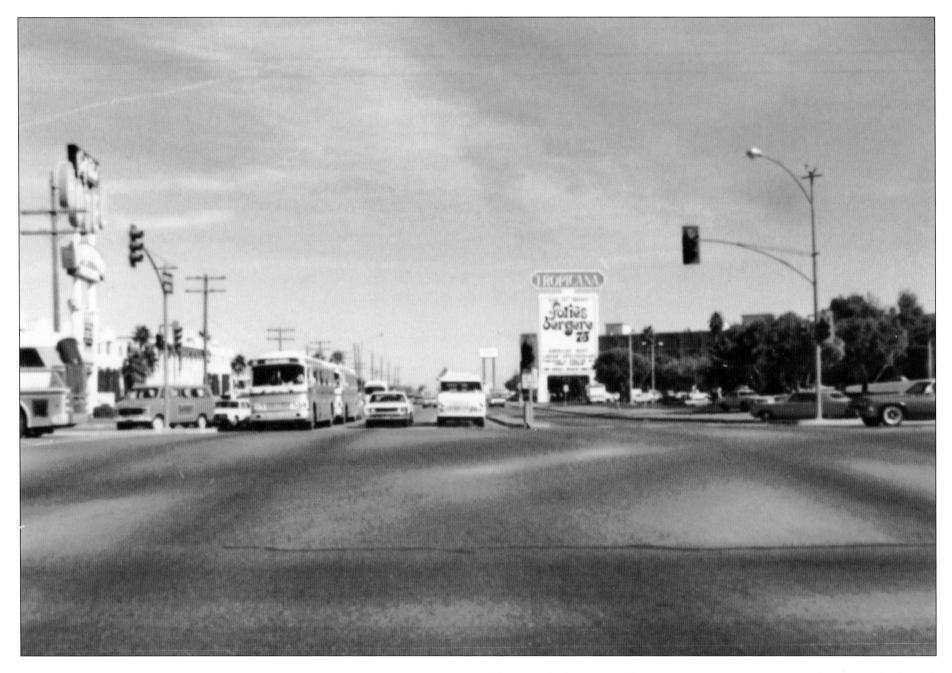

This view looks east on Tropicana at its intersection with Las Vegas Boulevard in 1975: the Tropicana Hotel sign advertising *Folies Bergere 75* is the most distinctive landmark on the quiet corner. Just out of sight, on the northeast corner, is the Marina Hotel. With the exception of the Tropicana and the distant Hacienda, the southern portion of the Strip had yet to match the development north of Flamingo Avenue.

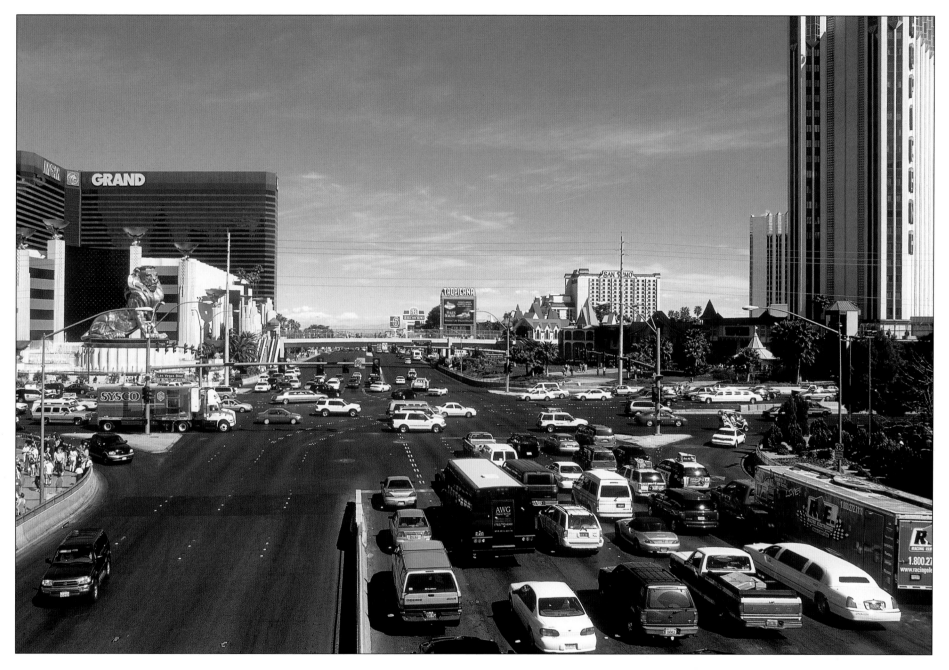

The majestic signature MGM lion—at forty-five feet tall and fifty tons, the largest bronze sculpture in the United States—sits perched atop a twenty-five-foot pedestal, surveying his domain. Built on the former site of the Marina Hotel and Tropicana Country Club by billionaire Kirk Kerkorian's MGM Grand, Inc., the hotel was completed in 1993 at a cost of $1 billion.

The MGM Grand's 5,000-plus rooms once made it the world's largest hotel. The First World Hotel in Malaysia currently holds that title, though Dubai has plans to surpass it with a $27 billion resort project known as the Bawadi project. The Bawadi project will house thirty-one hotels in an effort to boost Dubai's tourism industry—without casinos.

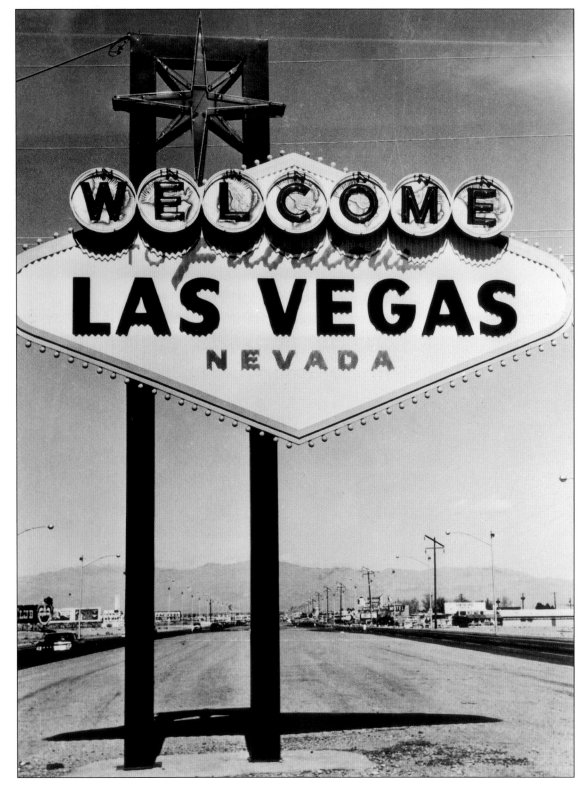

A view of the "Welcome to Fabulous Las Vegas Nevada" sign looking north on the Strip in 1969 shows a background of billboards and tiny motels in the distance. One of the most recognizable symbols of Las Vegas, the sign was designed by Betty Willis, a commercial artist, and created by Western Electric Display in 1959.

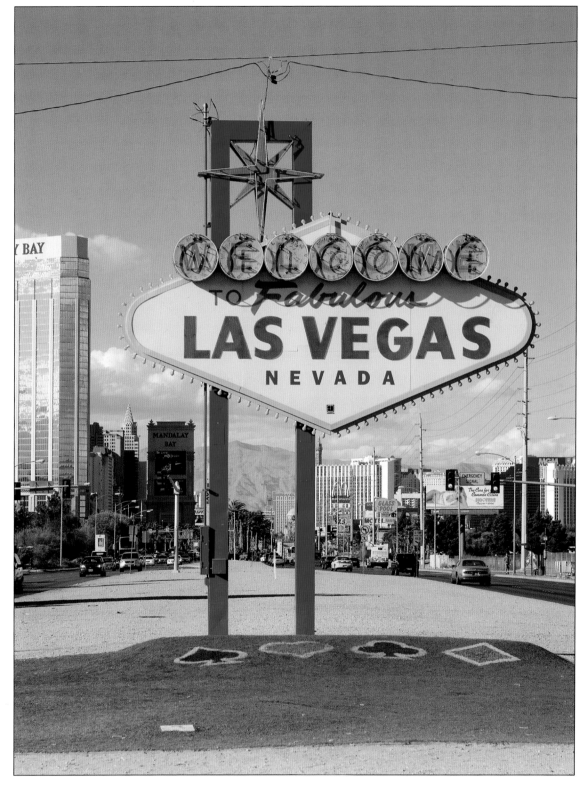

The "Welcome to Fabulous Las Vegas Nevada" sign looks the same today, but the backdrop on the Strip has changed dramatically. In the distance, a vista of high-rises populate Las Vegas Boulevard, the most prominent being the golden tower of the Mandalay Bay Hotel. The sign itself has become such a Las Vegas icon that it was chosen to adorn the city's official centennial license plate and is featured on the "Welcome to Nevada" U.S. postage stamp.

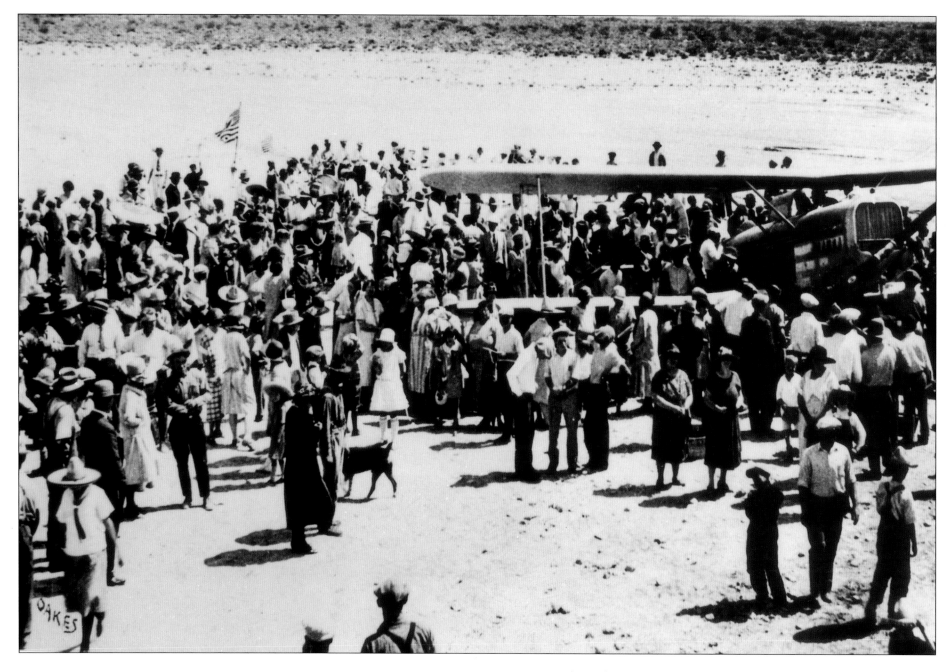

Las Vegas residents throng Rockwell Field as the Western Air Express plane inaugurating regular contract air mail service to the city arrives on April 17, 1926. Located at the corner of what is now Sahara and Paradise, Rockwell Field was the second airfield in Las Vegas; the first flight into Las Vegas had landed near what is now Las Vegas Boulevard and Stewart in May 1920.

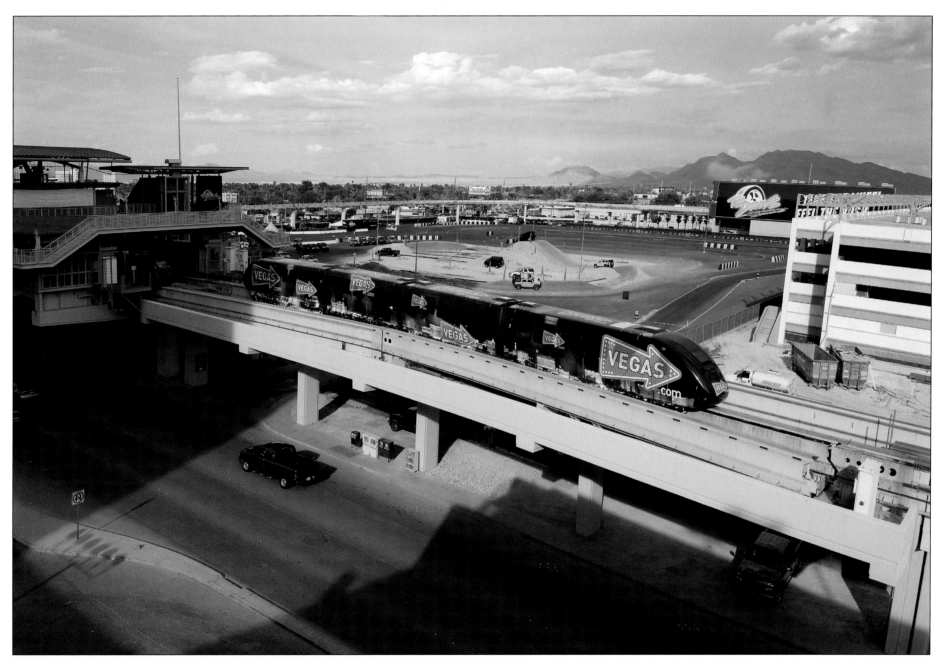

By the 1930s, Western Air Express had outgrown the landing space and facilities available at Rockwell Field; it was abandoned after the company purchased land for a new airfield at the site of the current Nellis Air Force Base. The Sahara Hotel parking lot now rests on this historic field and, as seen in this picture, is framed by the monorail track that stretches four miles, past the convention center and all the way down to the MGM Grand. The monorail began service in 1995, and can get one to practically any major destination on the east side of the Strip via six different stations. A three-day pass costs less than $50 and includes service until as late as three in the morning.

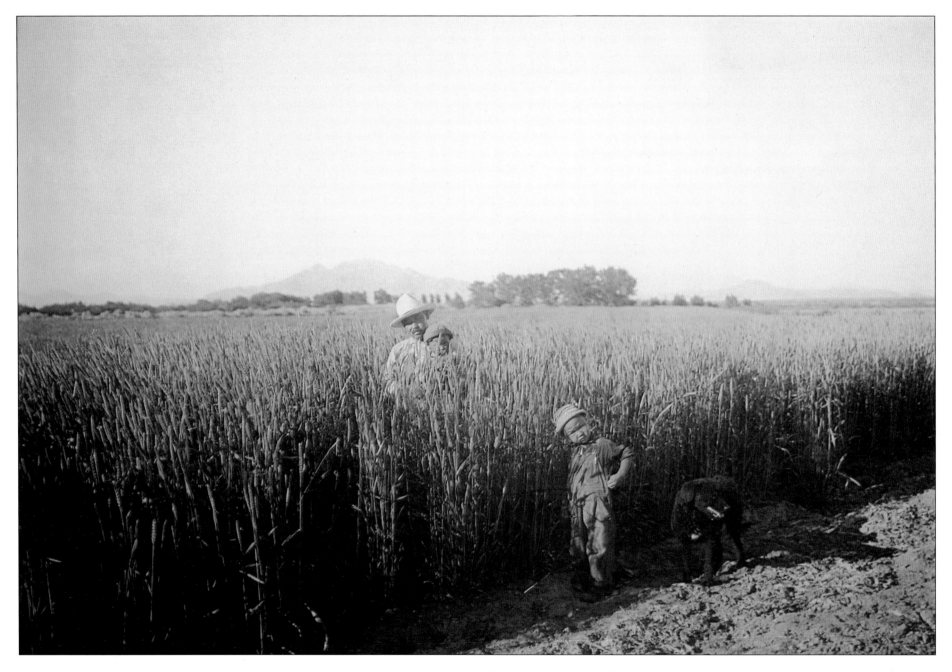

Far from the bustle of Fremont Street and the Strip, the 160-acre Tomiyasu Farm flourished in the vicinity of what is now Pecos and Warm Springs Road from the 1920s to the 1960s. Owner Bill Tomiyasu, shown here in 1923 with his children, grew a wide variety of fruits and vegetables. At its peak in the early 1930s, the farm supplied tons of produce to Six Companies, Inc., to feed workers at the Boulder Dam construction site.

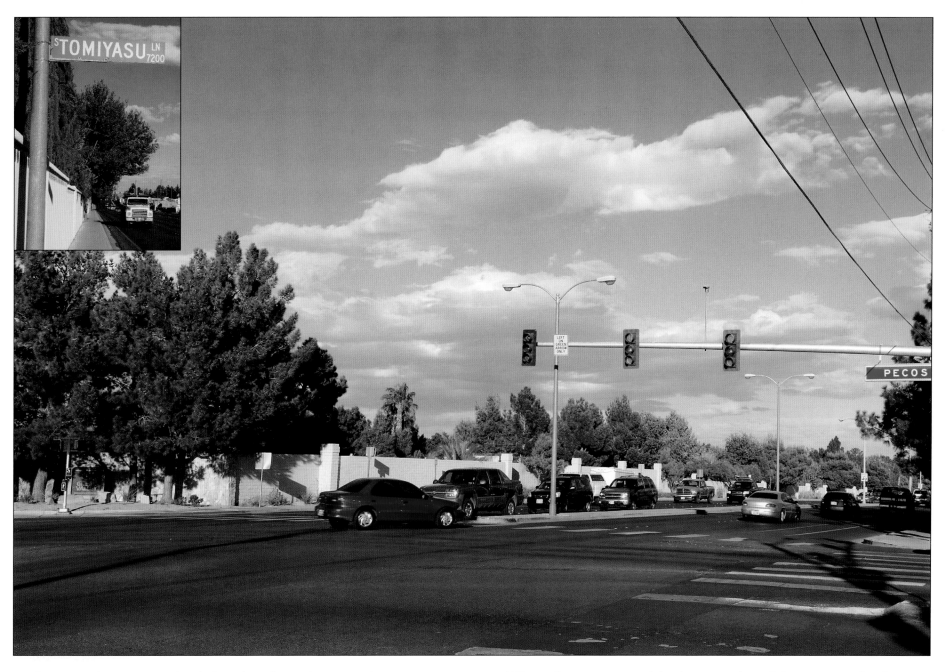

In the 1960s the Tomiyasu family lost their farm after a set of circumstances resulted in a controversial foreclosure that made Las Vegas headlines. The ranch house was torn down and the valuable property was subdivided and sold. Gated, multimillion-dollar homes now cover the area where fields of produce once flourished. Tomiyasu Lane (*inset*), located just west of Pecos

and Warm Springs, is one of the few reminders of the Tomiyasu family legacy in this area. However, the botanical legacy the Tomiyasus left on Las Vegas can be seen all around in the various types of flora that the family helped to cultivate.

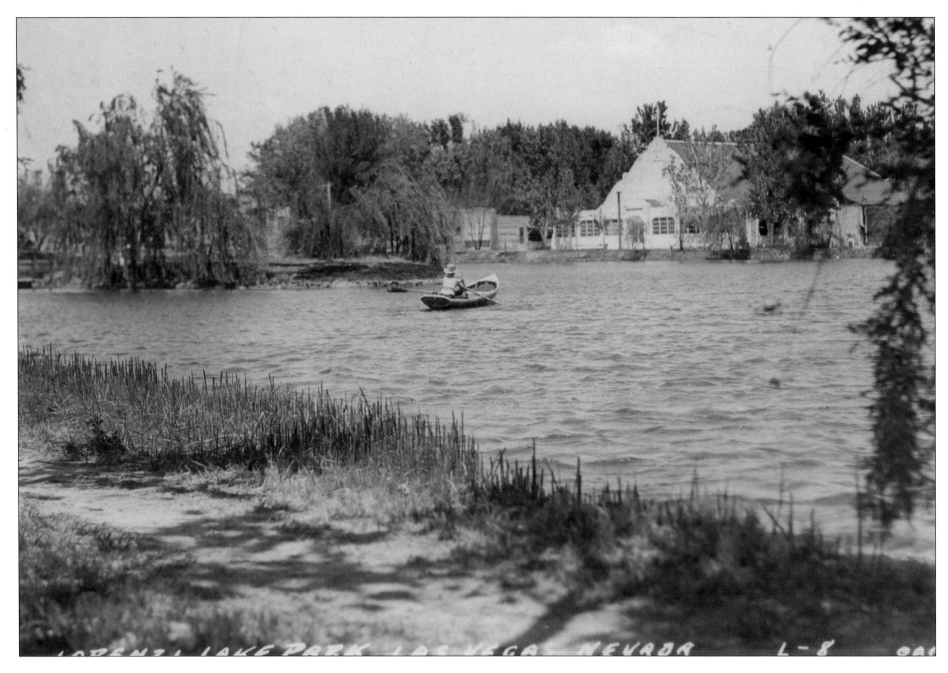

Shade trees cluster along the banks of the lakes at Lorenzi Park looking toward the dance pavilion in this view from the early 1930s. The resort was opened in May 1926 by French immigrant David Lorenzi about two miles west of the town center, and consisted of two man-made lakes with islands in the center, a dancing hut, and a spring-fed swimming pool. Lorenzi stocked the lakes with bluegill, crappie, black bass, and large bullfrogs, and built a band shell with a movie screen on one island.

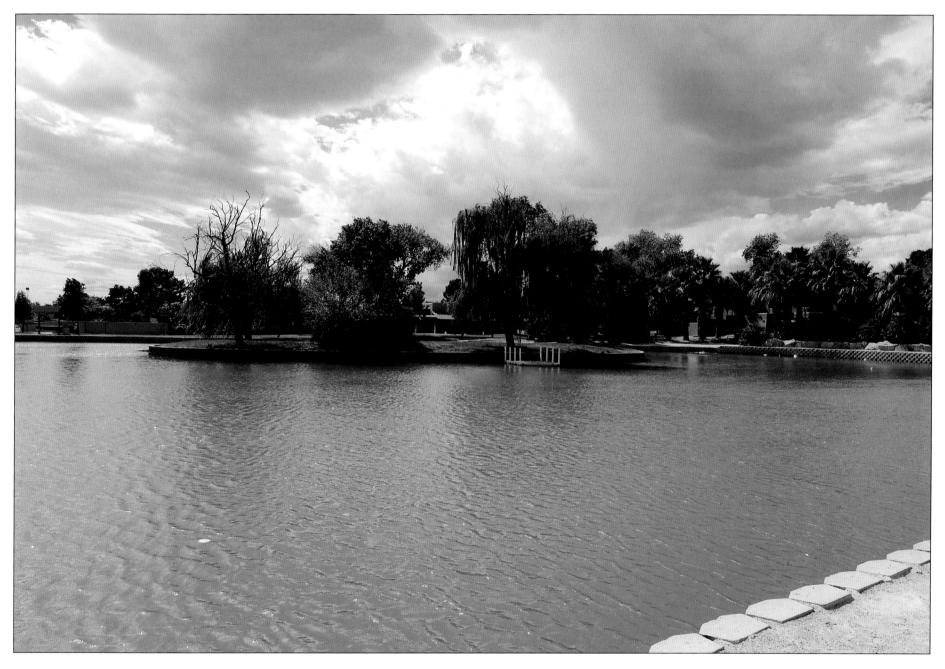

David Lorenzi had always wished his park could belong to the people, but city officials were not inclined to buy it, and the property was purchased by businessman Thomas Sharp in 1937. For ten years it degenerated into swamps before Lloyd St. John refurbished it into the popular Twin Lakes Lodge. The City of Las Vegas finally purchased the property in 1965. It is now a public park and is also home to the Nevada State Museum and Historical Society. The park's Sammy Davis Jr. Festival Plaza has become the de facto hub of operations for numerous events, from fun runs and festivals to school field trips every week. Of special note is the Autumn Arts Festival, which is sponsored by the Las Vegas Department of Leisure Services.

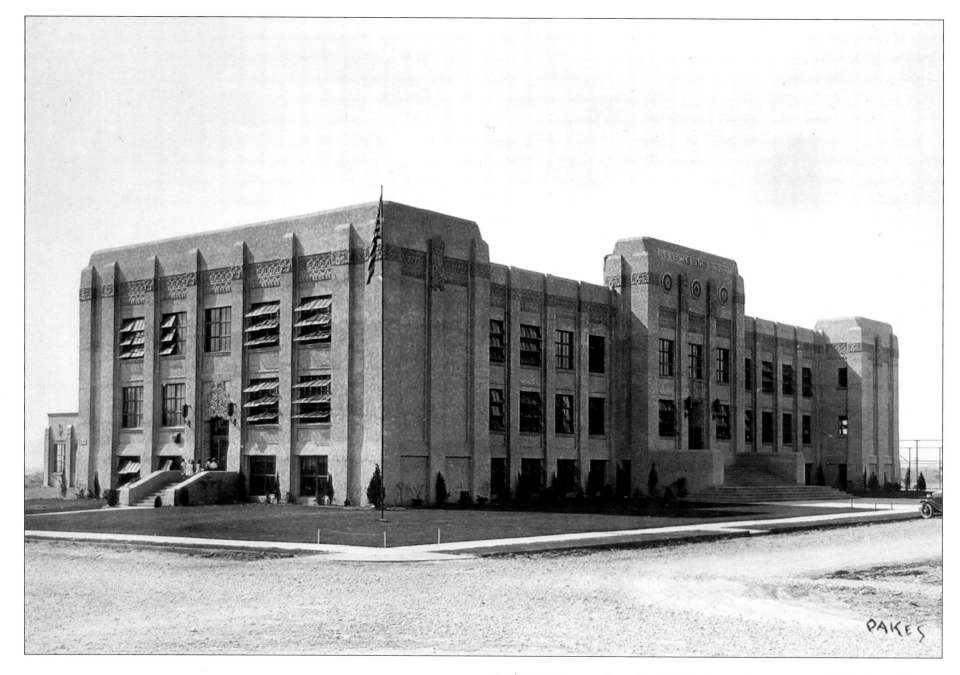

Built in 1930 to replace the old Mission-style structure on Fifth Street, Las Vegas High School was designed by the Reno firm of George A. Ferris & Son in a variation of Art Deco style described as Aztec Moderne. At the time, the school's location at Seventh and Bridger was criticized for being too remote, but fears that the school would never attract enough students were eased when it filled to capacity just two years after opening.

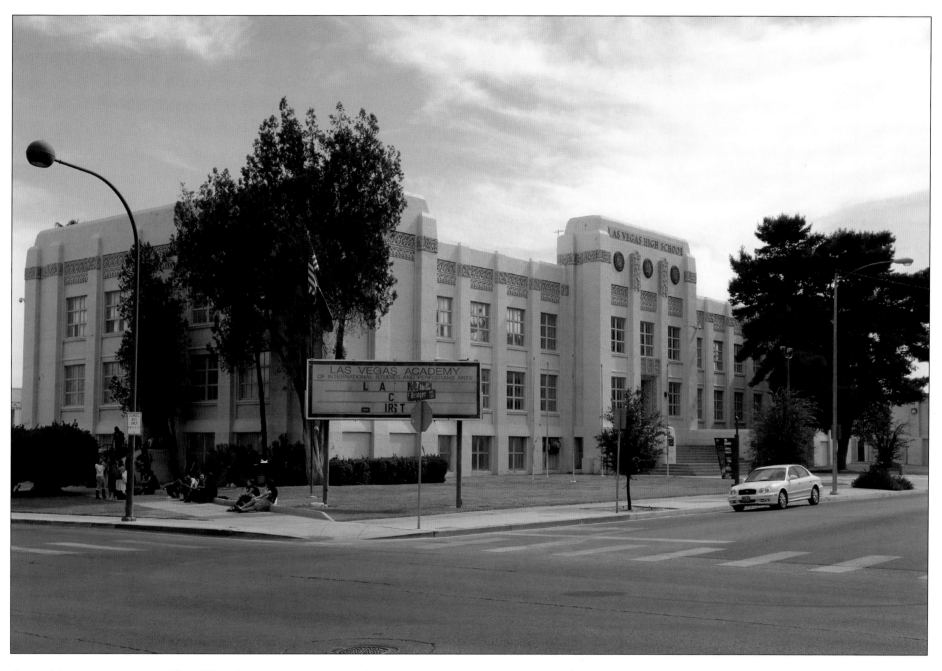

One of the success stories of Las Vegas historic preservation, the Las Vegas High School building was entered on the National Register of Historic Places in September 1986. In 1993, a new Las Vegas High School campus was constructed near the foothills of Frenchman's Mountain at the east end of Sahara Avenue, and the original building on Seventh Street became the Las Vegas Academy of International Studies, Performing and Visual Arts. In addition to stewarding the advancement of youth in the arts, the institution serves the community through live performances featuring tomorrow's superstars in this magnificent historic building. The school's theater put on its first production, *Anatomy of Gray* by Jim Leonard Jr., in 1995.

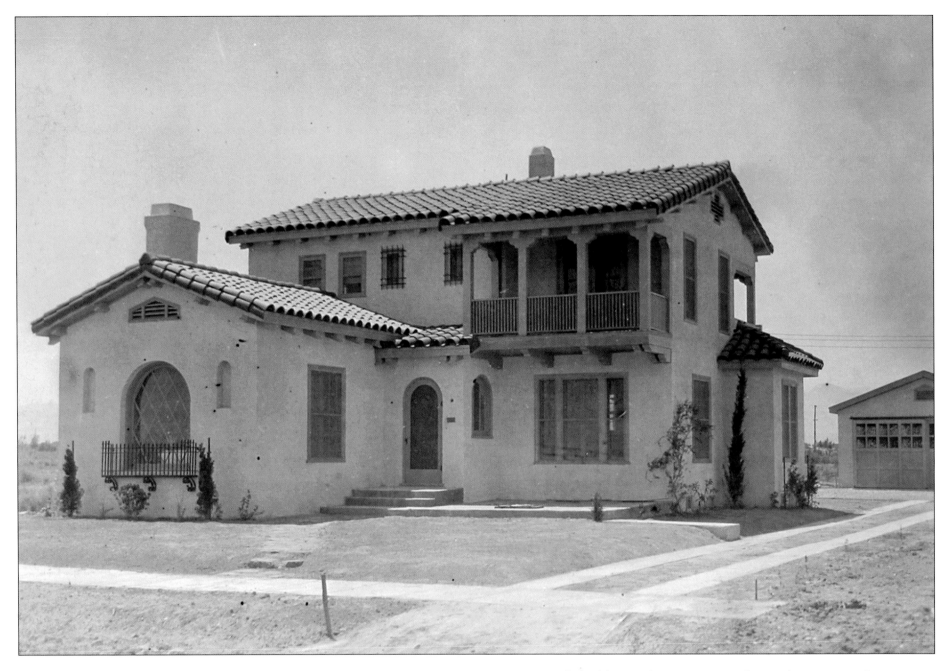

A Mission-style building in the Monterey tradition, this two-story home at 704 South Ninth was designed by Las Vegas architect A. Lacey Worswick, and was noted for its cantilevered balcony. It was built in 1930 at the considerable cost of $10,000 for A. S. Henderson, an educator and attorney who had served Las Vegas as superintendent of schools, legislator, and district court judge.

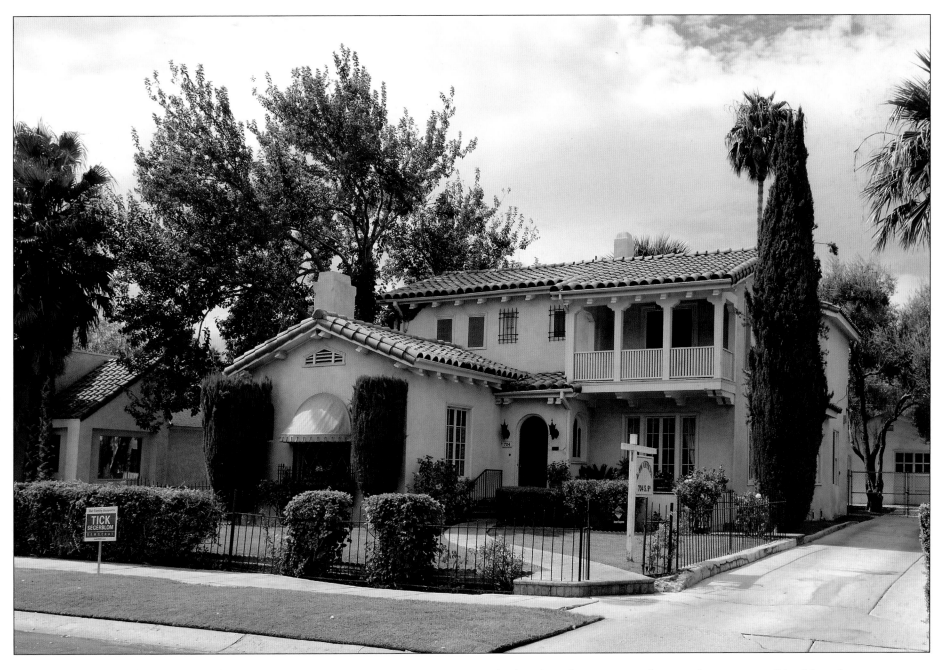

Lush landscaping now surrounds the Mission-style home on Ninth Street, but its exterior has changed little in seventy years. No longer a private residence, it now houses the law offices of Kermitt L. Waters and remains one of the architectural gems of the Las Vegas High School neighborhood.

The law firm that occupies this significant piece of Las Vegas history as its base of operations has served Las Vegas for over twenty-five years, specializing in eminent domain law. Most appropriately, a firm that protects the rights of land owners should have property that is worthy of preserving.

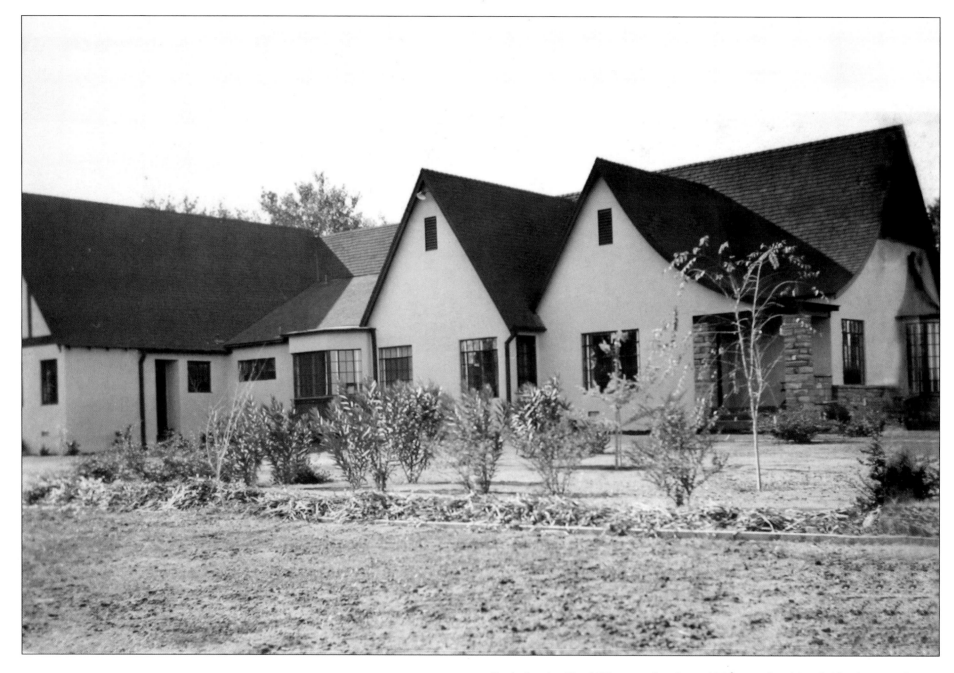

Built for the Cyril Wengert family in 1938 near Sixth and Charleston, this charming residence was one of many early Las Vegas homes designed in the Tudor-Revival style. Designed by Clifford Nordstrom, the home featured the picturesque gables with half-timbering typical of the Tudor-Revival style. Wengert, a Las Vegas pioneer and civic leader, led the First National Bank for many years, and later served as vice president of the Southern Nevada Power Company.

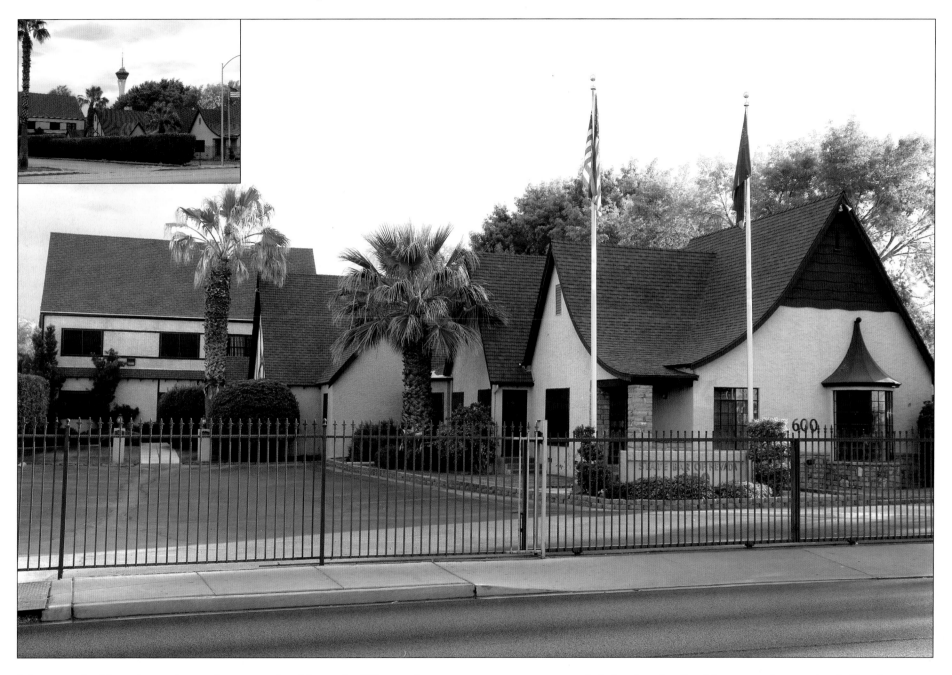

Like many buildings located near downtown Las Vegas, the Wengert house ceased to be a private residence long ago. In 1976, the Schreck law firm carefully restored the house, designing an addition that would blend in with the original structure. It currently serves as the office for the State Bar of Nevada. The Wengert name lives on today through the family's great work in commerce and philanthrophy; Las Vegas even has a school, Cynthia Wengert Elementary, named after a member of the prominent banking family. The Stratosphere Tower (*inset*) can be seen in the background. The tower's double-decker elevator lifts visitors to the top at 1,800 feet per minute—or three floors per second.

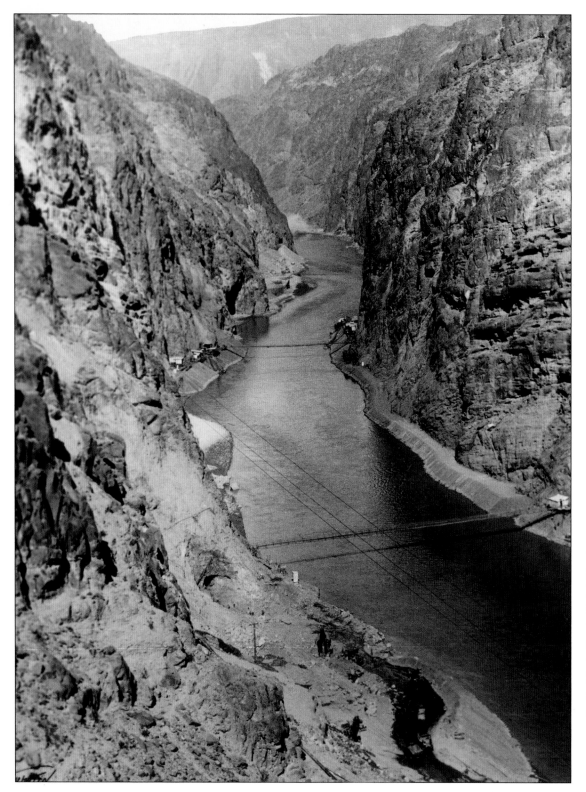

The solution to years of destructive flooding along the Colorado River, the construction of Boulder (later Hoover) Dam at a site just thirty miles outside Las Vegas was a boon to the local economy. Thousands of dam construction workers came to Las Vegas to spend their paychecks, and many more tourists came to view the construction site and visit the city that billed itself as the "Gateway to Boulder Dam." This view shows a pristine Black Canyon looking upstream in 1931 just prior to the beginning of construction on the dam.

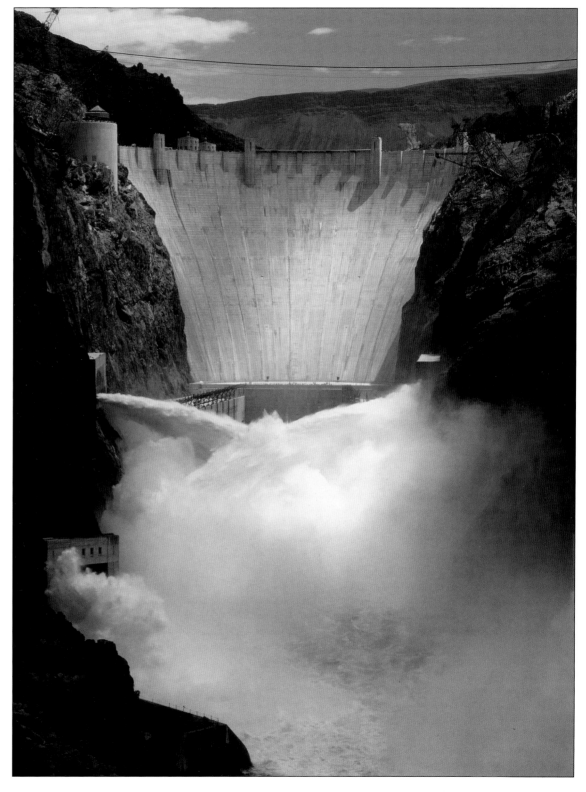

Completed two years ahead of schedule, Boulder Dam was dedicated on September 30, 1935, by President Franklin D. Roosevelt. In 1947, a Republican-controlled Congress acted to change its name to Hoover Dam in honor of the former president who had worked so diligently to ensure its construction. Over seventy years later, it remains a wonder of modern engineering, annually attracting a million visitors and generating four billion kilowatt-hours, enough to serve 1.3 million people. In 2006, $5.7 million was appropriated for maintenance and improvements to Hoover Dam and other dams in the area. PBS recently made an extensive feature film celebrating Hoover Dam as one of the greatest engineering works in history and for its role in transforming the face of the American Southwest.

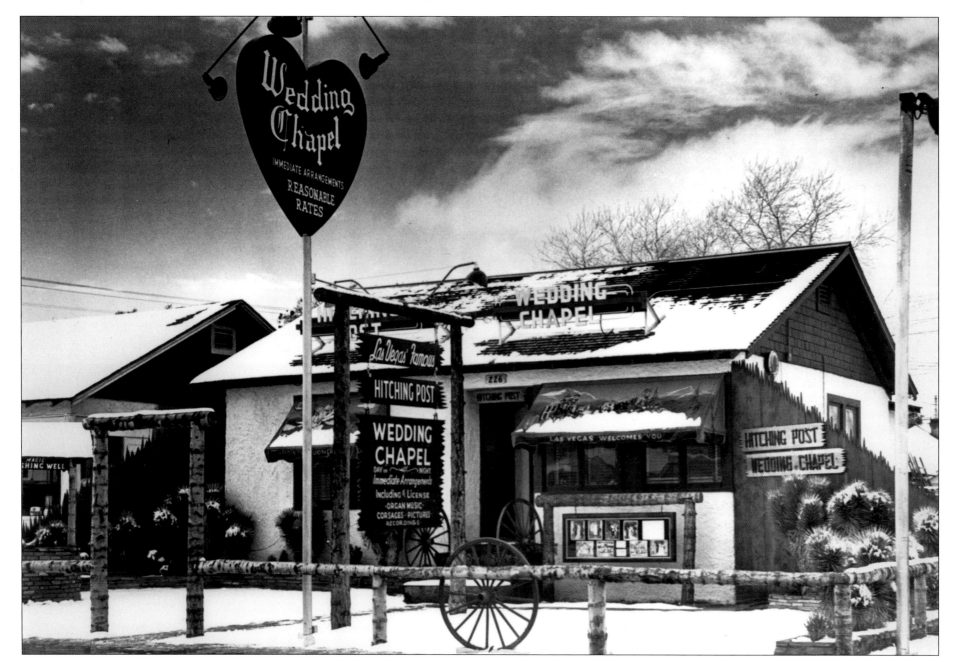

With Nevada's liberal marriage (and divorce) laws, Las Vegas has long been a popular wedding site for both celebrities and ordinary citizens who flock to the many chapels scattered along the Strip and downtown. One of the city's oldest wedding chapels is the Hitching Post, founded in 1926, which is shown here as it looked in its original location on 226 South Fifth Street in the late 1940s.

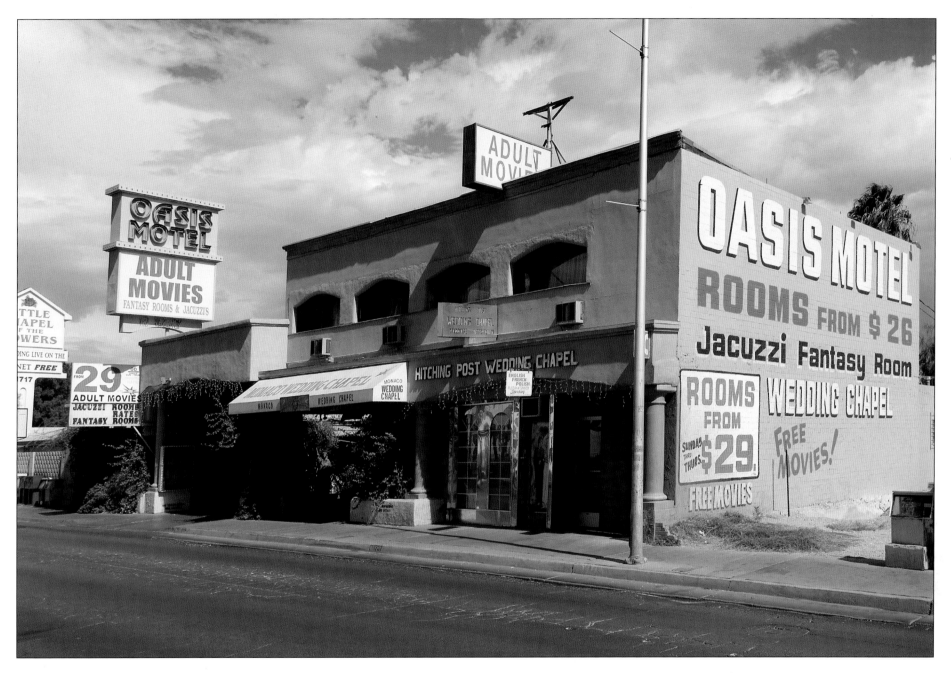

Today the Hitching Post appears overshadowed by its neighbor, the Oasis Motel, at its new location just north of the Stratosphere Tower. Although one in a string of wedding chapels located just north of Sahara, the Hitching Post's longevity makes it unique. Few, if any, other chapels can claim to have married the children and grandchildren of their original patrons. One can get a basic wedding package for less than $50 per couple, and the chapel will provide everything its clientele might need, from rings to flowers to veils. The Hitching Post was featured in the Elvis video *Viva Las Vegas*. When the wedding scene was filmed, many second-rate journalists reported that Elvis Presley and Ann-Margret had actually been married.

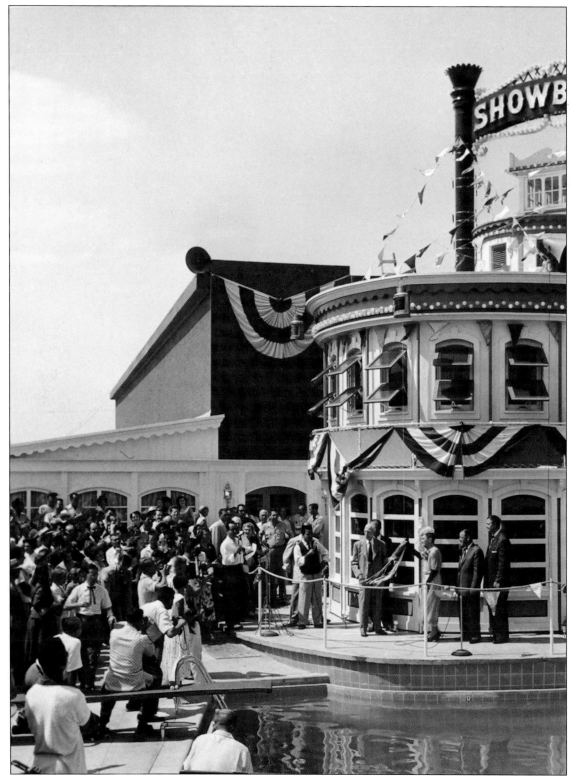

In this image, pioneer Las Vegas residents "Mom" and "Pop" Squires christen the new Showboat Hotel on its opening day, September 3, 1954. The nautical-themed hotel was designed to resemble an 1840s side-wheeler, with its prow jutting out into the swimming pool. Its location near the remote intersection of Fremont and Boulder Highway was carefully planned after contemporary surveys suggested that this area would soon be the new center of town.

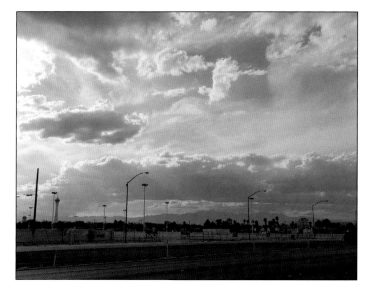

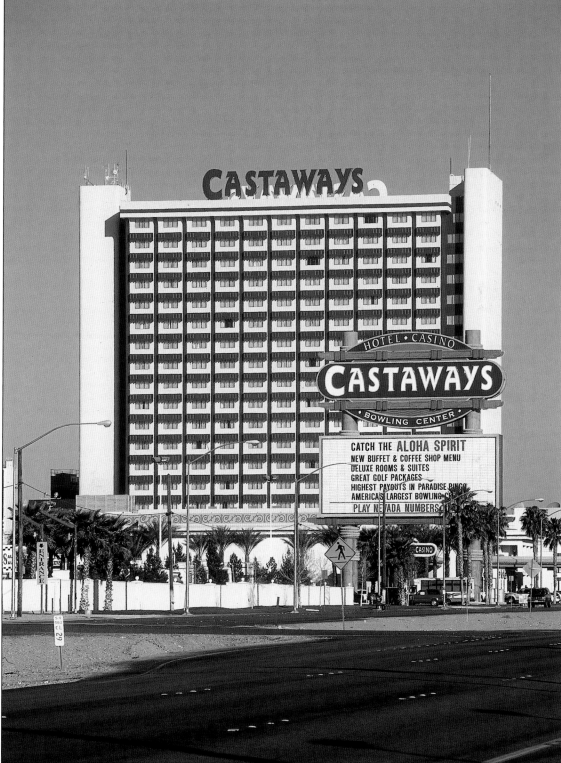

Although Boulder Highway never did fulfill its promise of becoming the new center of town, it did become home to a number of off-Strip casinos catering to locals by virtue of their food bargains and favorable gambling odds. The Showboat was particularly popular and successful because it operated one of the largest bowling centers in the West. Its original showboat exterior long gone, the resort was sold and reopened as Castaways in 2001. Things did not go well for the second generation of the Castaways name. By 2003, Castaways had generated more than $50 million in debt and was soon in bankruptcy. Station Casinos bought the twenty-six-acre site for $33.7 million in 2006 and the Castaways tower was imploded in that same year. The site currently sits vacant (*above*).

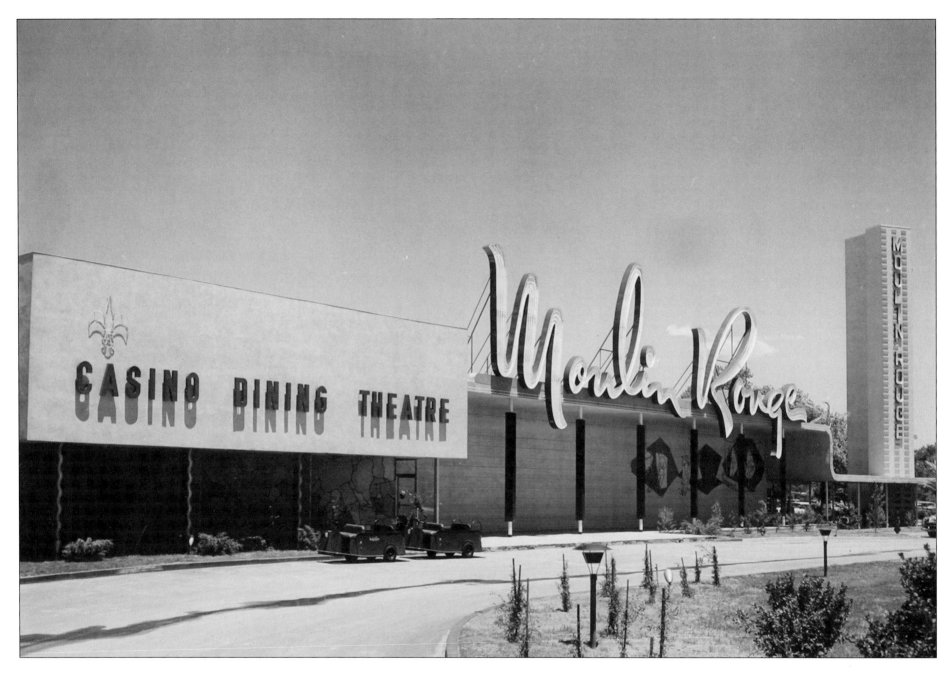

Frequently referred to as the "Mississippi of the West," Las Vegas was a deeply segregated town in the 1940s and 1950s. Black patrons were not allowed to enter most casinos on Fremont Street or the Strip, and black entertainers were often refused accommodation at the luxurious resorts where they performed. In May 1955, the elegant Moulin Rouge on Bonanza Road opened as the first interracial casino and hotel in Las Vegas.

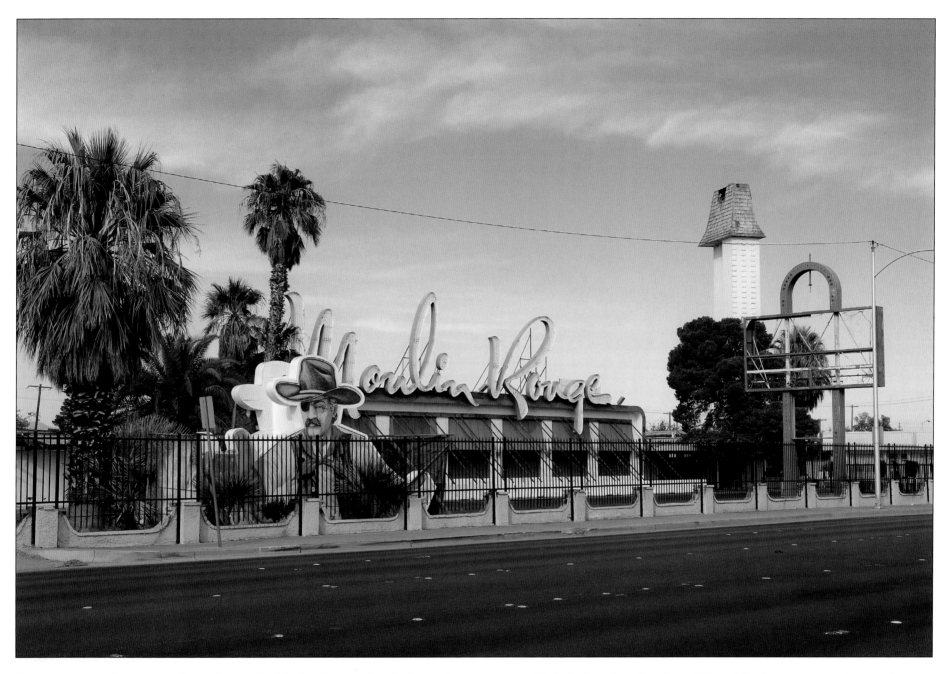

Despite its initial success and popularity, the Moulin Rouge closed after only six months due to financial mismanagement. Although it was entered on the National Register of Historic Places in December 1992, subsequent owners have met with little success in returning it to its former glory. Efforts to save the Moulin Rouge had been ongoing. In April 2002, the Preserve Nevada group added the hotel to their list of Nevada's eleven most endangered historical sites. But then in May 2003 a devastating fire—suspected to have been caused by arson—engulfed and destroyed the old building. While the building was burned, the facade of the building still remains—as do many fond memories of this off-Strip piece of Americana.

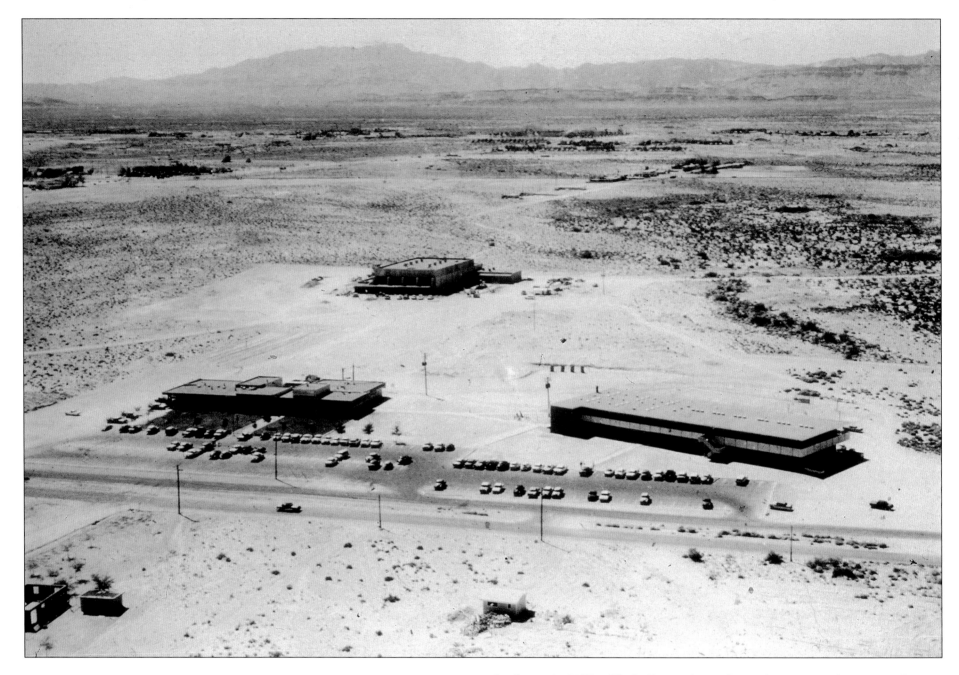

In the early 1950s, Clark County's rapid population growth prompted community leaders and educators to appeal to the University of Nevada regents in Reno for the establishment of an extension campus in Las Vegas. In 1957, Nevada Southern University was established on sixty acres in Paradise Valley, just two miles east of the Strip. An aerial view looking west around 1960 shows the Maude Frazier building (left), the Archie Grant building (right), and the new gymnasium (center).

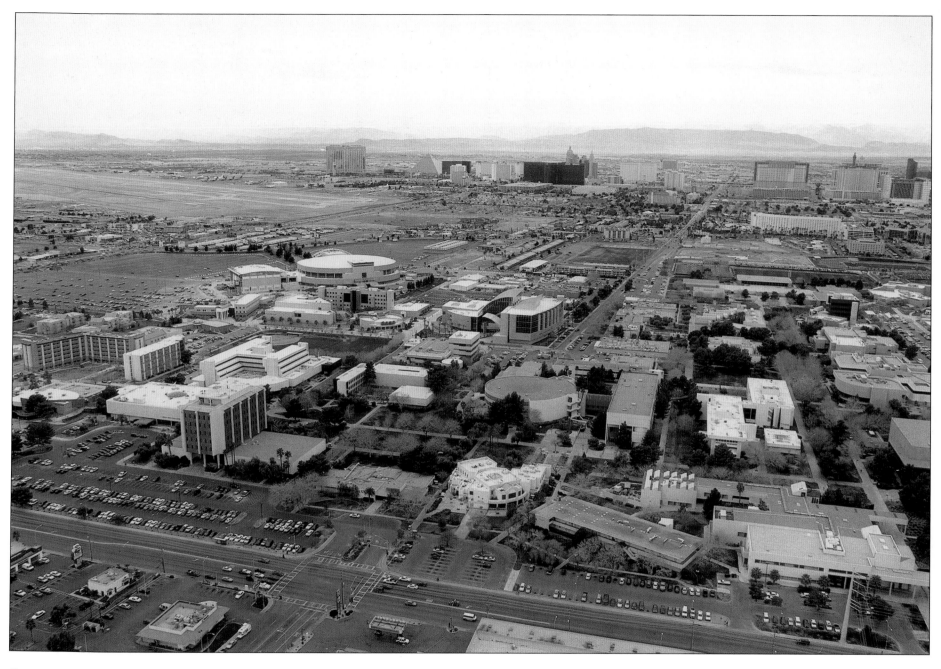

Sparse surroundings led some to nickname Nevada Southern University "Tumbleweed Tech" in its early years, but in 1969 the campus was officially designated the University of Nevada, Las Vegas. Although UNLV initially had a strong athletic focus, recent years have seen it develop into a research-oriented university. Dramatic growth over the years has enlarged the campus significantly, as can be seen in this modern aerial view. The university has seen significant growth, both physically and in terms of ambition, since its early days. As a matter of fact, 2006 saw the first global branch institution of UNLV with the opening of a branch school in Singapore. The institution operates out of Singapore's National Library Building and houses a number of fields of study, including, most appropriately, the William F. Harrah College of Hotel Administration.

INDEX